Praise for The Hamster Revolution

"Simple but powerful. This is life-changing stuff."
—Chris Granger, Vice President, Team Business Development, National Basketball Association

"Our daily barrage of email not only consumes our time and energy but fills up our in-boxes with someone else's priorities. These simple tools will allow you to reclaim your life."
—Betsy Myers, Executive Director, Center for Public Leadership, Harvard University

"A must-read for every employee I supervise. You'll love it!"
—Richard L. Andersen, CFE, Executive Vice President, San Diego Padres

"Great stuff! This book delivers simple and practical email management protocols."
—Paul Roithmayr, Director, Organization Development & Training, 20th Century Fox Film Corporation

"A clever way to add fifteen days to your year."
—Joe DiDonato, President, ESource Corporation

"A powerful new strategy for email efficiency and etiquette."
—Lamonte Thomas, Vice President of Sales and Customer Relations, Cigna

"These email practices will change the way you work."
—Matt Koch, Director, Productivity & Knowledge Management, Capital One

"A home run! Find time for what matters most. For example, taking your family to the ballpark!"
—Rick Mears, Vice President, Guest Services, San Francisco Giants

"Cut through email clutter and take control of your life!"
—Lisa Lelas, author of *Simple Steps: 10 Weeks to Getting Control of Your Life*

"A refreshing and humorous approach to reducing email overload. We use the insights every day."
—Steve Stone, CEO, Infoflows

The Hamster Revolution

How to Manage Your Email
Before it Manages You

The Hamster Revolution

Mike Song
Vicki Halsey
Tim Burress

Berrett–Koehler Publishers, Inc.
San Francisco
a BK Life book

Patent Pending COTA System - CKS dba getcontrol.net

Berrett-Koehler Publishers, Inc.
235 Montgomery Street. Suite 650
San Francisco, CA 94104-2916
Tel: 415-288-0260   Fax: 415-362-2512   www.bkconnection.com

Ordering Information

Quantity sales. Special discounts are available on quantity purchases by corporations, associations, and others. For details, contact the "Special Sales Department" at the Berrett-Koehler address above.

Individual sales. Berrett-Koehler publications are available through most bookstores. They can also be ordered direct from Berrett-Koehler: Tel: (800) 929-2929; Fax (802) 864-7626.

Orders for college textbook/course adoption use. Please contact Berrett-Koehler: Tel: (800) 929-2929; Fax (802) 864-7626.

Orders by U.S. trade bookstores and wholesalers. Please contact Ingram Publisher Services, Tel: (800) 509-4887; Fax: (800) 838-1149; E-mail: customer.service@ingrampublisherservices.com; or visit www.ingrampublisherservices.com/Ordering for details about electronic ordering.

Berrett-Koehler and BK logo are registered trademarks of Berrett-Koehler Publishers, Inc.

Printed in the United States of America

Berrrett-Koehler books are printed on long-lasting acid-free paper. When it is available, we choose paper that has been manufactured by environmentally responsible processes. These may include using trees grown in sustainable forests, incorporating recycled paper, minimizing chlorine in bleaching, or recycling the energy produced at the paper mill.

Library of Congress Cataloging-in-Publication Data

Song, Mike, 1964-
   The hamster revolution: how to manage email before it manages you / by Mike Song,
      Vicki Halsey, and Tim Burress.
      p. cm.
   Includes bibliographical references.
   ISBN: 978-1-57675-437-5 (hardcover)
   ISBN: 978-1-57675-573-0 (pbk.)
   1. Electronic mail messages –Management. 2. Personal information management. I. Halsey,
      Vicki, 1955-II. Burress, Tim, 1964-III. Title.
      TK5105.73.S66 2007
      651.7'9 —dc22   2006024284

First Edition
14 13 12 11 10   15 14 13 12 11 10 8 9 7 6 5

Producer: Tolman Creek Design Copy Editor: Patricia Brewer, Proof Reader: Ginny Munroe, Indexer: Shan Young

The productivity of knowledge work — still abysmally low — will become the economic challenge of the knowledge society. On it will depend the competitive position of every single country, every single industry, and every single institution within society.

—Peter Drucker

Every generation needs a new revolution.

—Thomas Jefferson

For Kristin Song, Richard Halsey, and Daphne Burress

Thanks for believing.

Contents

Foreword

Every once in awhile, the business world teeters off balance. This usually happens when events converge to create an absurd situation or *incongruity*. Invariably, an *incongruity* is a big opportunity. In the 1980s, the incongruity was that managers lacked a simple system for managing people. When the rubber met the road, most lacked the people skills needed to maximize performance. Along came *The One Minute Manager®* and suddenly millions of professionals had a book that *simplified the management of people*. Twenty years later, I'm thrilled that it continues to help managers manage and leaders lead.

In the 1990s, the *incongruity* was that people lacked a simple strategy for managing change. This was absurd because the '90s were a time of great upheaval in the business world. Along came Spencer Johnson's *Who Moved My Cheese?®* and suddenly millions of professionals had a book that *simplified the management of change*.

Today, the *incongruity* is that you're asked to process more information, particularly email, than is humanly possible. Each day you multitask your way through an avalanche of disorganized, unstructured information. It's a stressful world filled with uncertainty and interruptions. That said, I have some very good news. Just when you need it most, along comes *The Hamster Revolution* with four highly effective strategies for *simplifying the management of information*.

You'll love this book for three reasons:

1. **It Works:** *The Hamster Revolution* contains practical and proven insights that will make you more effective the next time you sit down at your computer.

2. **It's a Valuable Guide for Leaders**: Email now consumes a quarter of the day for the typical professional. If you aspire to be a great leader or team player, you have to develop a strategy for managing email. *The Hamster Revolution* provides clear guidance on how to do just that.

3. **It's Fast and Fun:** Let me guess—you're busy, right? Sometimes you barely have time to think, let alone read a long book filled with thousands of tips. Relax. You can read this book in about 90 minutes. The authors focus on "a *small number* of *high-impact* email insights." You're going to smile when you meet the book's star: Harold. He's a funny guy and in some ways, he'll remind you… of you.

I'd like to congratulate you for being here, right now in this moment. You've envisioned something that many of your colleagues and competitors have yet to discover: *You can't unlock your fullest potential when you and your team are drowning in email.* It's time to address the *incongruity* of email overload. It's time for the next big revolution to begin. So cue the lights and quiet on the set. Here comes Harold and *The Hamster Revolution*!

Ken Blanchard
Co-author, *The One Minute Manager*®

1

CONFESSIONS OF AN INFO-HAMSTER

I was working peacefully in my office when the door slowly opened and shut with a click. I looked up but no one was there. "You'd better be able to help me!" said a small voice. *Was this a joke?*

I stood up and *that's* when I saw him. Trudging across the floor, tugging on his tie, was a small, nervous-looking white hamster with brown spots. He was wearing a dark blue business suit and carrying a small black briefcase. He looked tired and defeated.

"I hear you're the so-called productivity expert," he said. "I'm Harold."

I leaned down to shake his paw, "Pleased to meet you, Harold. And yes, my passion is helping professionals lead more productive and fulfilling lives."

Harold raised his eyes hopefully. "Maybe I'm in the right place after all," he muttered.

Once I'd gotten over my initial shock that Harold was a hamster, I realized that he was my 1:30 PM appointment.

"Welcome, Harold! Please sit down and tell me what brings you here."

Harold hopped into a chair facing my desk. As he leaned back, his wireless personal digital assistant (PDA) buzzed loudly. Harold looked down at it, lost his balance, and almost fell through the gap in the back of the chair. He scrambled frantically to keep from falling and eventually regained his composure.

"Okay, okay. Here's my story. Five years ago, I landed my dream job: Human Resources Director at Foster and Schrubb Financial. At first, the position was perfect. I was incredibly productive and my team launched several big initiatives." Harold frowned and shifted in his seat, "But a couple of years ago, I noticed that I was working harder and harder and getting less and less done."

"How'd that feel?"

"Am I in analysis or something?" quipped Harold, rolling his eyes. "Well, Dr. Freud, I felt stressed. I was getting buried alive by email, voice mail, and meeting notes. I had information coming out of my ears."

Harold pointed at the PDA clipped to his belt. "Then I got this thing. At first I liked being connected 24-7, but soon I fell even further behind and…"

"Yes?"

"To make matters worse," Harold said softly as he picked at some loose fur on his wrist, "and this is embarrassing to admit," he leaned forward and whispered, "Lately, I'm having trouble finding stuff."

I leaned forward and whispered, "What kind of *stuff*, Harold?"

"Well, I'll store an email and when I really need it — I can't find it! Things just vaporize! And don't get me started on my team's shared storage drive; everyone's storing documents differently; no one knows how to clean it up; it's a mess! I spend a lot of time requesting resends and recreating documents that are missing. I'm staying late just to keep up."

"So work is spilling over into your personal life?"

Harold raised his furry eyebrows thoughtfully. He reached into his pocket and produced an impossibly small picture. I squinted and saw that it was Harold's family: a lovely wife and two beautiful children.

"Nice family."

"Upset family," corrected Harold wearily. "Thanks to wireless technology, I'm always online. Carol's really frustrated with the amount of time I spend working after-hours."

He held up his paws with an exasperated look. "The kids hate it when I do email on Saturday or Sunday. But part of me actually looks forward to weekends just so I can catch up on work. Sometimes, I miss a soccer game or dance recital but if I don't keep up…" Harold shrugged his little hamster shoulders as if to say, "*I just don't know anymore.*"

"So your dream job's become a nightmare?"

Harold nodded. "I feel like I'm losing… me."

He continued quietly, "I used to love learning new things. I was thrilled to get to the office each morning. Now I dread it. I feel like… like…" Harold struggled for the right words.

"Like a hamster on a wheel?" I offered.

"Yes!" shouted Harold, bolting upright in his chair, "I've become a *hamster on a wheel!* Running faster and harder, but getting nowhere."

I suddenly realized that Harold was unaware that he'd actually turned into a hamster. Although I'd helped countless professionals who felt and acted like hamsters, Harold was the first that actually *changed* into one! Apparently his metamorphosis had been so gradual that he hadn't noticed.

Harold paused and let out a deep sigh. "When I was younger, I had a much different vision of how my life would unfold."

"Tell me about that."

Harold raised his eyebrows and stared at the ground. He looked like he was trying to recall a distant memory.

"Well, I dreamed I'd have this really fulfilling job. I pictured myself surrounded by brilliant people working on these high-level, high-impact team projects — exciting stuff, life-changing stuff. I also imagined that I'd have much more time with my family, to laugh with friends, work out, garden, reflect." Harold smiled wryly, "I never thought I'd spend every waking hour stressing over email and feeling like a hamster on a wheel."

2

A NEW WAY TO WORK

Harold raised his paws in frustration. "So you're the expert. How do I get off the wheel?"

"You fight back, Harold. There's a better way to work."

"Yeah, yeah," he said looking tense, "I've taken a couple time-management classes, but they didn't help."

"Harold, this isn't a *time*-management problem. It's an *information*-management problem."

"It is?"

"Yes! Too much email and information is gushing into your life. Don't get me wrong; email is an amazing communication tool. But suddenly, it's keeping a lot of people from getting things done. Most professionals feel like they're stuck on a nonstop wheel-of-information overwhelm."

"So what's the answer?" asked Harold, sounding frustrated.

"Join *The Hamster Revolution*."

"Huh?" asked Harold looking surprised. "Revolution against what?"

"Info-glut!" I said. "That's your enemy: way too much low-value information mucking up your world. You can't reach your fullest potential when you're drowning in email! *The Hamster Revolution* is a strategic plan that helps you conquer info-glut once and for all. Interested in learning more?"

"Sure," said Harold, looking both interested and worried at the same time.

I handed Harold a single sheet of paper, "Here's our schedule."

The Hamster Revolution Plan

Week 1 (Today): Email Insights (90 Minutes)

    Strategy 1: Reduce email volume

    Strategy 2: Improve email quality

    Strategy 3: Coach others to send you more actionable email

Week 2: Information Storage Insights (60 Minutes)

    Strategy 4: File and find info fast with COTA©

Week 3: Wrap-Up Meeting (30 Minutes)

Harold studied the schedule and seemed pleased, "Three hours works for me. I don't have a lot of time for this."

I nodded. "Today, we'll focus on streamlining the flow of email through your life. This will help you become more relaxed and effective at work. Sound good?"

"Wonderful, if I could actually do it," replied Harold cautiously.

"Don't worry. Our goal today is to concentrate on a *small* number of *high-impact* email insights. By the way, you won't have to write anything down because each Hamster Revolution strategy will be summarized by an easy-to-use tool."

"Four strategies and four tools… that's good," stated Harold emphatically. "But what exactly is next week's meeting about? What is COTA?"

"A moment ago you mentioned that you were having trouble finding things?"

"Sure."

"What if you could file and find all of your email, documents, and links in a flash?"

"That would be a miracle," said Harold softly.

"I can't promise you a miracle, but I've seen amazing results from people who've adopted an organizational system called COTA. COTA is a simple yet effective way to arrange your files and folders. After the COTA session, we'll give you a week to put all four strategies into practice on the job. During that week, you can call me anytime for coaching or feedback. Okay?"

Harold thought for a moment, "Seems like a workable plan so far."

We'll hold a third and final wrap-up meeting to see how you did. We can fine-tune your newly found Hamster Revolution skills and answer any lingering questions."

Harold leaned forward, "So it's kind of like a one-two punch? First we get email under control, and then we use this COTA thing to organize my information?"

I nodded. "We've discovered that there's a powerful *connection* between email efficiency and the way you store your info."

"What kind of connection?"

"Here are just a few examples:

- Reduced email volume means less email to store.

- Clear email subject lines make it easier to relocate stored email.

- A highly effective folder system helps you rapidly file email and documents. This reduces inbox overload.

- Responding to an email requesting info is a lot easier when you can find your info fast.

- There's also a time connection. Together, email and information storage tasks consume over 40% of a typical professional's day. [1, 2] When both of these activities become more efficient, your overall productivity takes a giant leap forward."

Harold raised his eyebrows. "So I need to improve *both* email and information storage to get off the hamster wheel?"

I nodded. "We're going to get your life back, Harold."

"I'll believe it when I see it," said Harold. "But I like your approach. You're looking at the whole process of managing information, not just email by itself. I've never thought of it that way before."

"You're not alone. Most professionals lack an effective plan for managing all the information flooding into their lives. To make matters worse, over the past five years, the volume of information we process has skyrocketed. For example, email volume is rising at a rate of 14.6% per year." [3]

Harold groaned, "I'm doomed."

"As inboxes and computer filing systems have become bloated, millions of professionals have begun to feel like hamsters. *Well, it's time for the hamsters to fight back!* The Hamster Revolution will restore order and control to your life. Best of all, it will save you 15 days a year."

Harold looked surprised, "15 days?"

"You can save a lot of time by mastering the flow of information through your world. So what do you think?"

Harold reflected on his predicament for a moment. Suddenly, with a determined look, he blurted, "Okay, I'll join your Hamster Revolution!"

"*Our* revolution," I smiled, "Ready to reclaim your life?"

Harold stood up on his chair and gave a mock salute. "Let the revolting begin!"

3

EMAIL ADDS UP!

As Harold saluted, Emilio, our Senior VP of Finance, walked past my door. His mouth dropped as he spied a tiny, saluting hamster teetering on a chair. He was so distracted that he crashed into a bank of filing cabinets, making a loud noise. Hoping that Harold wouldn't notice, I launched into one of my favorite topics: The True Cost of Email Overload.

"I love coffee, Harold. To be specific, I love Blue Sky mochaccinos, an irresistible blend of coffee, cream, and rich chocolate."

"We have a Blue Sky Café in our building, too," said Harold, looking confused.

"Well, several years ago I noticed that I was buying two or three cups of coffee a day. We were trying to trim the family budget so that we could save for our kids' college education. Just for kicks, I decided to calculate what those mochaccinos were costing me. It was more than $3,000 a year! Over time, I was literally spending my kids' college tuition on coffee!"

Harold shot me a look that said, "*What does this have to do with email?*"

"Email is a lot like coffee, Harold. It's kind of addicting and it definitely adds up."

"Addicting?" asked Harold, looking puzzled.

"Has your email system crashed in the past year?"

Harold nodded. "I did have a problem last month and it felt terrible. I was petrified that I was missing something important and I felt totally cut off from the world. I was really cranky and — looking back — I completely overreacted."

"The symptoms you describe sound like what I experience when I don't get coffee for a couple days. Those are feelings of withdrawal, Harold. Email occasionally brings us exciting and important information. Perhaps those emotional highs trigger something in our minds that makes us want to check it all the time."

"Sometimes I wind up doing email even when I have much more important things to do," noted Harold.

"Exactly, another reason we default to email is that it's easy and nonconfrontational. It's easier to zip off a critical email than it is to conduct a difficult live conversation with a colleague who is underperforming. Don't get me wrong. Email is a great productivity tool, but we're overusing it and in some cases — we're abusing it."

"Never thought of it that way," agreed Harold.

"Do you know how much email costs you each year?"

"Well isn't that the beauty of email? It's free. No stamps!" smirked Harold.

"We'll see," I replied. "How much time do you spend on email each year?"

Harold shook his head, "I have no idea. I guess I get about 50 a day and I probably hit the *Send* button about 25 times."

I slid a calculator across my desk. "So you send and receive a total of 75 emails per day. Let's calculate your annual email volume: Multiply your 75 daily emails by 240, which is the number of work days per year. What do you get?"

Harold raised his eyebrows in wonder. "I process 18,000 messages per year? Wow."

"What else do you do 18,000 times a year?" I asked.

Harold paused, "I don't know... maybe breathe?"

"Right," I said, "next to life-sustaining activities, email may be what we do most."

"Ughhh," Harold groaned.

"We practically live for email and that's why we've got to do a better job of managing it. How much time do you think you spend on email each day, Harold?"

"I'm not sure, but I would guess at least two and a half hours."

"So it takes you 150 minutes to process 75 emails a day. That's an average of 2 minutes per email. Now multiply your 18,000 annual emails by 2 minutes to get the total number of minutes you spend on email each year."

Harold did the calculations and stared in disbelief, "36,000 minutes per year?"

I nodded and leaned forward. "Now divide by 60 minutes to get the total number of hours you spend on email each year."

Harold was even more dumbfounded. "600 hours per year? No wonder I can't get anything done!"

"Now divide by 8 hours to calculate the number of 8-hour workdays you spend on email each year."

"I spend 75 workdays per year on email? That's almost four continuous months of email a year! Can that be right?"

Harold was stunned. He did the calculation again and came up with the same number. Looking up he mused, "And this doesn't even include the email I do during holidays, vacations, and weekends."

I nodded and paused a moment to let it all sink in. "Let's cut to the chase, Harold. What percentage of the time that you spend on email is *wasted*?"

"Where do I start?" said Harold with a grimace. "People constantly send me long, unnecessary, and convoluted messages. I get copied on everything. *Reply-to-all* is out of control."

Harold paused to calm down and then blurted, "At least a third of the time I spend on email is poorly utilized or wasted!"

I nodded. "If you spend 75 days a year on email and a third of that time is wasted…"

Harold looked up in amazement. "Then I'm wasting 25 days a year on email?"

"That's more than a month of your career up in smoke each year. Using an average salary of $30 per hour, the cost of 25 wasted days is roughly $6,000 per worker each year or $6,000,000 for a company with 1,000 employees!"[4]

Slowly Harold reasoned, "So email isn't free at all. In fact, it's one of the *most* expensive things we do at Foster and Schrubb."

"And yet, you've received little or no guidance on how to manage it effectively," I guessed.

"That's true," said Harold quietly. At that moment, I noticed a change sweep over Harold's face. Suddenly, he looked more present and energetic.

Harold shot me a determined look. "Okay, Coach, teach me how to get my time back."

I grinned and said, "Okay. Now let's see — our goal is to reduce your annual email processing time by 20%. Because you spend 75 days a year on email, this equates to a savings of approximately 15 days. To achieve this goal, you'll need to change the way you think about email. Are you prepared to make some changes and leave your comfort zone, Harold?"

"I'll leave the planet to get back 15 days!" stated Harold firmly.

How Much Time Could You Save By Reducing Email by 20%?			
Emails Sent and Received Each Day	**Annual Emails**	**Days Spent on Email**	**Days Saved with 20% Reduction**
20	4,800	20	4
30	7,200	30	6
40	9,600	40	8
50	12,200	50	10
60	14,400	60	12
70	16,800	70	14
80	19,200	80	16
90	21,600	90	18
100	24,000	100	20

"Good," I smiled. "One more thing, Harold. How will you spend those 15 days?"

Harold thought for a moment, "Hmmmm. Not sure..."

I pushed a paper and pen across the table. "Take a moment and write down two important things you'd like to accomplish with 15 extra days over the next 12 months. Basically, 15 days a year equates to two and a half hours a week. Choose one personal and one professional goal. If you don't create a concrete plan for the time you'll save, you'll just wind up running harder and faster on the wheel."

"I'll default to email," acknowledged Harold. He thought for a moment and then wrote:

- *Personal: Take Kyle to karate two nights a week.*
- *Professional: Implement Accountability Training Program.*

Harold and I took a moment to discuss his goals. Apparently his 8-year-old son Kyle had been struggling with his grades and a certain bully at school. Kyle had expressed an interest in martial arts, but Harold, busy as always, hadn't followed up. As Harold discussed his son's struggles, I sensed that spending more time with him could make a big difference.

Harold also explained that Foster and Schrubb needed to develop a training program that promoted accountability. As the company had grown, lines of responsibility had become fuzzy. Many of Harold's co-workers failed to take ownership for key projects and decisions. Internal and external client satisfaction was dropping each quarter. Ironically, Harold had been tasked with creating an accountability program, but he had failed to follow through.

"I just couldn't find the time," he shrugged.

"I like your goals," I said. "They're realistic and attainable. Let me double-check something with you. Do they motivate you? Will you build them into your schedule in order to make them happen?"

"Absolutely," said Harold with conviction.

Reader Exercise: What personal and professional goals could you accomplish by joining the Hamster Revolution?

Hamster Revolution Goals	
Goal	**Type of Goal**
1.	Personal
2.	Professional

4

STRATEGY 1: REDUCE EMAIL VOLUME

Once Harold had chosen his goals, we began work on reducing his email volume.

"Okay, Harold, let's start with the simplest and most overlooked email reduction technique: *Send Less — Get Less.*"

Harold shot me a look of disbelief, "How does sending less help? I mean, my problem is that *other* people send *me* too much email."

"At first glance, it doesn't seem like we have much control over email overload. But a closer look reveals something very different. Research shows that for every five emails you receive, three require a response.[5] This means that for every five emails we send, people send back three. I call this the boomerang effect. So if you eliminate just one out of every five outgoing emails, you'll begin to receive roughly 12% fewer emails."

"Plus I'd save the time it takes to create one in five outgoing emails," added Harold thoughtfully. "But, I'm pretty sure that most of my outgoing email is necessary."

"I agree," I said with a nod. "But *most* isn't all. I'd be willing to bet you a coffee that 20% of your email doesn't actually need to be sent."

"I'll take that bet," grinned Harold. "But I'm not sure how you're going to prove it."

"Let me give it a shot," I replied. "How do you feel as you process email each day?"

Harold thought for a moment. "Lately, I feel uptight. I have a knot in my stomach. I worry that I've missed some critical email buried deep in my inbox. Maybe that's why the unnecessary emails I get are so distracting and frustrating."

"Sounds stressful," I commented.

"It is. I usually have just a few minutes between meetings and I'm dashing off messages to colleagues on my PDA. I try not to miss anything urgent. Back at my desk, if I have some spare time, I usually dive in and try to delete or respond to as many emails as possible. At home, email is always on my mind. I'm constantly sneaking off to check messages and hammer out a few replies. When the kids catch me, boy, do they get mad!"

"It sounds kind of hectic and reactive."

Harold nodded. "With lots of interruptions. Your hamster wheel is a perfect analogy. Most of the time, I'm on auto-pilot: *Open–Read–Reply, Open–Read–Reply, Open–Read–Reply…*"

I nodded. "When we're stretched too thin, and primarily reacting to one interruption after another, we tend to send *me-mail*. Me-mail is all about rapidly clearing out *our* inboxes and pushing out lots of *our* information. It's all about me, me, me. Maybe that's why email has become an increasingly mindless process. We're losing track of what our recipients want and need. Vague, incomplete, and redundant messages are excellent examples of me-mail."

"Okay, but I don't think I'm sending me-mail it's mainly my co-workers," protested Harold.

"Initially, the vast majority of the professionals we've encountered feel just like you. But our research has revealed an interesting twist: 79% of the professionals we surveyed believe that their *co-workers* often overuse *Reply-to-all.*"

"You've got that right!" laughed Harold.

"…Only 13% believed that they, *themselves*, overuse *Reply-to-all.*"[6]

Harold stopped laughing and thought for a moment. "I guess when we're overwhelmed, it's easier to blame others versus taking responsibility. It's harder to ask, 'What's *my* role in creating this challenge?'"

I nodded. "And that's understandable. Just as new parents don't get an owner's manual, professionals receive very little coaching on email."

"Very little?" smirked Harold. "I haven't received any!"

"Have you ever *provided* email feedback to your colleagues?"

"Not really," admitted Harold with a shrug. "It's something we've never addressed at Foster and Schrubb. I guess we think, 'How tricky could email be?' We're supposed to be thinking about the bigger strategic things."

There was a long pause as something registered in Harold's mind. Slowly he reasoned, "Because we don't get any feedback, maybe we're all doing what we *think* works best instead of what actually *does* work best. Maybe we're missing a big opportunity to lighten our collective load."

"Exactly," I said, "In my experience, everyone has a different idea about what constitutes a necessary email. To reduce email volume, you need a simple, mutually agreed upon tool that clearly defines for everyone what should and shouldn't be sent."

"Oh, I love software," replied Harold. "Tell me I can download something to fix this mess."

I sighed. "It's not software, Harold. It's *headware*! It's a tool that sits up here." I tapped my forehead with my index finger, "In your mind, that helps you stop sending unnecessary email. This tool helps you to stop and ask three important questions before hitting *Send*."

Harold shot me a skeptical look. "Okay, what are these three magical *Ask Before You Send* questions?"

"Here you go," I said handing a small laminated card to Harold. "We call this the 1-2-3 Email Quantity Tool. It's going to save you a lot of time."

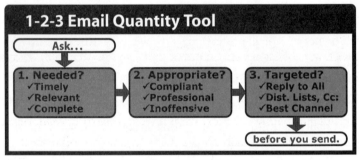

Harold twitched his whiskers as he examined the simple diagram on the card, "How does this work?"

"Before hitting *Send*, ask: Is my email (1) Needed? (2) Appropriate? and (3) Targeted? Let's take them one at a time."

Question One is:

1. NEEDED?

(Does my busy recipient truly *need* this email to do his or her job?)

"If you take a moment to visualize your email recipient struggling through a typically busy day with a bunch of meetings and 100 emails in his inbox, you'll find yourself sending fewer and fewer unnecessary messages. You begin sending *we-mail* instead of me-mail. *We-mail* is information that is truly *needed* by the recipient in order to do his or her job. It's specific information for a specific purpose."

"I wish my colleagues sent more of that," laughed Harold, "Maybe I wouldn't be drowning in email."

"And perhaps," I offered gently, "Some of your colleagues wish that *you* considered their needs more carefully before hitting *Send*. Being judicious with email actually shows that you care for and respect your co-workers. Let me give you a few examples of email that isn't needed:

- **The FYI Light Email.** Many messages are sent because a sender suspects that *someone* on their team may *some*day be able to use *some* aspect of a particular piece of information. Many busy professionals find that they no longer have the time to read and store lengthy FYI light emails. In the future, tie every outgoing email to a *specific* business need.

- **The Trivial Thank You Email.** We all want to be polite. But trivial thank-you emails for routine tasks are becoming a pet peeve for a growing number of business people. It's one more unnecessary interruption in a workday already filled with interruptions. Has this ever happened to you? You're working on an important project that requires a lot of concentration…

your masterpiece… and ding, an email comes in. Someone is thanking you for sending the weekly report, which is something you do every week, and poof — you lose your train of thought?"

"Oh yeah, all the time," agreed Harold, "And sometimes, I never get back on track."

"Me either. In the future, in order to reduce email overload, the standard will be to reserve thank-you emails for extraordinary efforts. If you absolutely have to thank people frequently, consider showing your appreciation at your next meeting or as a part of a brief greeting in a more necessary email.

- **The Redundant Email**. When news breaks, we all want to pass it along. But too many times the same message is trumpeted around an organization by 17 different colleagues. Before sending an email, always consider whether someone else *has* or *will* be sending the same content.

- **The Incomplete Email**. In the age of wireless, handheld PDAs, it's tempting to send a series of partial replies to a single request. For example, sometimes we quickly send back a short acknowledgement or partial answer via PDA. Then, just a little while later, when we return to our computer, we send a second more robust reply. This is just one kind of incomplete email that drives recipients crazy because it takes time to piece together both replies. A better strategy is to wait until you're back at your desk and send one complete message to your recipient.

- **The Email Containing Searchable Info**. In the past, we understandably wanted to share every piece of useful information we encountered with our colleagues. Today, a growing percentage of that information is easily found on the Internet via keyword search and other web-based services.

For example, I no longer need people to email me directions because I can find them online in a flash. So before sending this type of info to my colleagues, I ask, 'Will my recipient store this piece of information or are they likely to search for it online?' If I think they'll search, I don't send it."

Harold was thinking. "I don't consider my recipients' needs that much. Sometimes I think, 'Hey, maybe Sue could do something with this' or 'Perhaps Ralph would get a kick out of that,' but I don't think about their busy lives, jammed inboxes, or the direct relevance of my message to their jobs."

"Would you be willing to take a look at some of the emails you've sent over the past few weeks?" I asked motioning toward Harold's laptop. He opened his laptop and pointed to his email.

"Have at it."

We spent the next 15 minutes filtering through Harold's last 30 emails.

"Okay, that one, that one, and that one," said Harold, pointing at his Sent Box with a shrug. "I'll admit that my colleagues didn't really need those."

Some of Harold's unnecessary emails were chatty and others contained outdated or redundant information.

He scratched his ear and took a deep breath. "So maybe I could cut back a little on unneeded email. But 3 out of 30 isn't bad, is it?"

"What do you think?" I asked with a smile. "That's a 10% reduction in outgoing email."

"Okay, I get it, email adds up. What's the next email reduction question?" asked Harold eagerly.

"*Ask Before You Send* Question Two is:

2. APPROPRIATE?
(Is this email compliant, professional, and inoffensive?)

"Eliminating inappropriate email is another way to drive down email volume while also reducing legal risk. Professionals often forget that email is *company property* that's stored forever and can be reviewed at anytime."

"Yeah, but who could possibly watch all the email streaming through Foster and Schrubb?" asked Harold. "Talk about a boring day job…"

"On a day to day basis, it's difficult. But IT departments are beginning to install software that can flag certain keywords and discussion topics. They can also retrieve any email you've ever sent in the event that a concern is raised."

"Well that's a scary thought."

"Well, you can't really blame them, Harold. As an HR pro, you know that companies have lost millions in legal penalties by failing to monitor inappropriate workplace behavior. The bottom line is that it's more important than ever to send email that's compliant, professional, and inoffensive."

"Could you be more specific?" asked Harold, "Getting sued is not on my to-do list."

"Sure:

> *A. Compliant.* Every company has an internal email policy. They also have to comply with various government laws. I'm sure that you don't knowingly send illegal email, but some messages fall into in a gray area. For example, you may be innocently asking about the legality of a particular action you're contemplating. I recommend conducting these kinds of communications face to

face rather than creating a permanent legal document that can be used in court.

B. *Professional.* Before sending a questionable email, ask yourself how you would feel if it appeared on the front page of a national newspaper. Would you look professional? If your email made an appearance on the evening news, would your company's stock price go up or down?"

"Wait a minute!" protested Harold. "If I send an email to my boss, how does it end up on the evening news?"

"Your boss could innocently forward it to someone she trusts. That person could send it on to 20 people. If one of those people has bad judgment or disagrees with the content of your email, then…"

"I'm sunk!" muttered Harold with a grim nod.

"I constantly remind myself that email is both *slippery and sticky*. It slithers and squirms into the oddest places and it *sticks* around forever. When it's unprofessional, it points a giant flashing spotlight back on you. That's why it makes sense to be more judicious and simply send less email. It's also important to make sure that outgoing email is completely…

C. *Inoffensive.* There appear to be no censors or barriers in the email world. Although it's a business tool, it has a personal feel. We speak our minds and that's Okay, as long as we don't cross a certain kind of line. The problem is the line between offensive and inoffensive is in the eye of the beholder. Because we aren't present when our outgoing email is read and we don't know who it might be forwarded to, we have no real control over who reads our email. So my recommendation is to keep jokes, wise words of wisdom, and emotionally charged emails to an absolute minimum because…"

"Uh, oh," interrupted Harold, "no jokes?"

I smiled. "I'd be *very* careful about jokes. Let's say you forward a joke about blondes and it gets into the hands of someone who's blonde who works with you."

"Er, not good," admitted Harold, folding his paws over his chest.

"The scary thing about jokes is that the more funny and cutting they are, the more likely it is that they'll be forwarded. If you send an offensive joke to 20 people who each distribute it to 20 people who all forward it on to 20 more people, that joke will be viewed by more than 8,000 people. If it contains streaming video and takes 10 minutes to read, then you just spent 1,333 hours of company time."

"All by forwarding one stupid joke?" reflected Harold.

"Possibly," I said. "Or maybe you just sent it to a trusted friend whose child happened to look over his shoulder."

"Never thought of that," mused Harold.

"Also be aware that *wise words of wisdom* messages are often hoaxes. Be suspicious of any urgent email that asks you to forward a message to everyone in your address book. In many cases, these emails have been crafted by people with ulterior motives. Let me give you some examples:

- **Penny Brown:** An email containing a vague plea to help an abducted child named Penny Brown asks you to forward her information and picture to everyone you know. Key dates, facts, and legal information are oddly missing. Sadly, this distracts attention from real missing children.

- **Celebrity Rants:** A harshly worded email, supposedly written by a famous newsman, indicates that he's suddenly changed his long-held political views. Surprisingly, he blasts people that he's spent a lifetime supporting.

- **Get Rich Quick:** An attorney asks you to forward an email from Microsoft to every person you know. In a generous move, Bill Gates has offered to pay you $250 for each person on your forwarding list."

Harold laughed, "Ugh. I've got to admit that I fell for that last one. I'm still waiting for my big check!"

"You're not alone. Millions of people forward these kinds of emails each day. When you do it, you waste everyone's time while undercutting your own credibility."

"Is there some way to know if I'm being hoaxed?" asked Harold.

"Yes. There are some excellent fact-checking websites such as Snopes.com."

Harold nodded and made a note of the site.

"One last thought. From time to time you'll be tempted to send an angry email. You may have every right to be upset with someone. But I strongly recommend using the *24-Hour Rule*. Feel free to write your email — sometimes it's healthy to acknowledge your feelings, but wait one full day before hitting *Send*. Ninety-nine percent of the time, you'll cool down and replace your angry email with a more professional message."

"The 24-Hour Rule," stated Harold with a sigh, "That's good advice. I've noticed a growing number of edgy emails being sent by my team. When we're under pressure, things seem to escalate and etiquette goes out the window. Sometimes those emails cause a lot of hurt feelings and resentment. One of my co-workers just got demoted because of an angry message."

I nodded, "It can be a career-limiting move. The bottom line is that you can save yourself and your associates a lot of time by sending only *appropriate* email that's compliant, professional, and inoffensive."

"Got it," nodded Harold. "So the first two *Ask Before You Send* questions make perfect sense: Only send email that's 1. *Needed by your recipient* and 2. *Appropriate*, which means compliant, professional, and inoffensive. What's the last one?"

3. TARGETED?
(Is my email being sent to the right number of recipients through the best channel?)

"Targeting is the most effective way to cut email time. The opposite of targeting an email is spraying it everywhere. Targeting your email means that you decrease the use of the three most powerful email distribution tools: *Reply-to-all*, *Cc:*, and distribution lists. Let's take a look at each one.

Limit Use of *Reply-to-all*

Reply-to-all is by far the biggest source of email complaints.[7] When senders use this tool, they make the *assumption* that everyone on a particular distribution list wants to engage in a spontaneous, virtual group discussion."

"Let me guess, bad assumption?" snickered Harold.

"Right. Invariably, many *Reply-to-all* recipients don't have the time to carry on that kind of conversation. But once a *Reply-to-all* is sent, many recipients feel *compelled* to join the discussion. An email sent to 20 people can quickly morph into 100 confusing and disjointed emails just because one person hit *Reply-to-all* and four others felt obligated to chime in.

Harold looked sheepishly at his computer and mumbled, "I've been known to chime in from time to time," he squeaked.

"And sometimes it's perfectly appropriate," I said earnestly, "But whenever possible, try to cut back. Don't use *Reply-to-all* for minor discussion points, chatter, or trivial thank you messages. If you must respond to a widely distributed email, consider replying *only* to the original sender. If it's an involved situation that requires team input, perhaps arranging a *synchronous* discussion at an upcoming live meeting or teleconference would save time and have greater impact."

"Synchronous?" asked Harold.

"A synchronous communication is a discussion in which people respond back and forth to each other in real time. People hate *Reply-to-all* because it creates a disjointed *asynchronous* group conversation. When a group of people respond at different times, it becomes very hard to follow the flow of the discussion. By contrast, a synchronous conversation at a live team meeting allows for discussion, input, and a clear final decision."

"I see your point, but how can I stop my teammates from hitting *Reply-to-all?*"

"When sending an email to a broad distribution list, you and your colleagues can include this verbiage:

To save time, please reply only to me rather than hitting Reply-to-all."

"That could work," agreed Harold.

"A final tip is to use NRN in the subject line when sending an email for which **N**o **R**eply is **N**eeded. Some teams have begun to use NTN – **N**o **T**hanks **N**eeded. Just make sure that your entire team understands what NRN and NTN mean."

"So you're pre-empting replies by typing in three little letters in your subject line," said Harold thoughtfully. "That makes a lot of sense."

"Right. Now let's move on to the *Cc:* and Distribution list tools."

Limit Use of *Cc:* and Distribution Lists

"Ten years ago, when email was just beginning to ramp up, we were all thirsty to be copied on every message. Times have changed. With the information age upon us, it makes good business sense to become more judicious with *Cc:* and distribution lists. We must constantly remind ourselves that *less is more*."

"Send Less — Get less," smiled Harold.

"Exactly. Remember to *Cc:* only those people who truly need to know. Complaints are growing from recipients who sense that they are being copied for the wrong reasons. Here are some examples:

- **Self-Promotion:** Copying a leader to show you're working hard or late
- **Manipulation:** Copying a colleague for political vs. business reasons
- **Humiliation:** Copying someone unnecessarily on an email in which the recipient is criticized or disciplined
- **Duplication:** Copying an associate to further document something that was already clearly documented

Overuse of *Cc:* can make a sender appear insecure, self-serving, and inefficient."

"Not a great way to build your professional image," quipped Harold.

"Finally, use distribution lists sparingly and create sub-distribution lists whenever possible. Ask to be taken off any distribution list that's no longer relevant to your job."

Harold glanced at his computer and gave me a guilty look. "I suppose you want to see if I've abused any of these targeting features?"

I nodded. As we combed through Harold's last 30 outgoing emails, we found four instances where Harold had used *Reply-to-all* when it really wasn't needed. He had also copied a number of people unnecessarily on several other emails.

"Four *Reply-to-alls* out of 30 emails isn't too bad," said Harold defensively.

"But Harold, you replied to an average of 15 people each time. That means that you actually created 60 additional unnecessary outgoing emails! Not to mention all the responses it triggered."

"Okay, Okay!" said Harold, raising his paws defensively, "I get your point: Minimize use of *Reply-to-all, Cc:,* and distribution lists."

"There is one more thing you can do," I said.

"Lay it on me, Coach."

"Carefully consider the communication channel through which you're sending your message. Before sending an email that's likely to result in a long back and forth discussion, carefully consider arranging a live, *synchronous* conversation instead.

"People should just pick up the phone!" exclaimed Harold.

"True," I said, "but keep in mind that 70% of all business phone calls[8] are now answered by machines."

"And now you're playing *asynchronous* telephone tag!" groaned Harold.

"Right. Too often we default to email because it's easy and we're in the habit of doing email. But the easiest channel isn't always the best channel. We need to invest more time in arranging discussions."

"So the key is to *schedule* a live conversation versus trying to get it all done via email or voice mail?" asked Harold.

"You bet. I also recommend exploring Instant Messaging (IM) as a way to conduct productive synchronous discussions. A person can reply to an instant message even when they're wrapped up in a phone call or meeting. They can respond by typing: "I'm in the middle of something, but I'll IM or call you back in 15 minutes. You can even set your IM profile to indicate if you're busy or available."

"So the key is to use IM to increase the amount of valuable synchronous dialogue versus frustrating asynchronous email threads and telephone tag?" asked Harold.

"Right."

"There's one small problem," said Harold sheepishly. "I have no idea how to use our corporate IM system."

"Some companies are holding back on IM. But if Foster and Schrubb offers IM, your IT team or a knowledgeable teammate can show you the ropes. Remember, IM should be used judiciously and only when you need a back and forth dialogue. When overused, IM simply creates more interruptions and busy work."

"I'll keep that in mind," said Harold. "There are so many ways to communicate these days," he mused, looking a little overwhelmed.

"You bet, Harold. That's why we constantly have to ask, 'Is this the *best channel* for my message?'"

I pointed at the 1-2-3 Email Quantity Tool: "Much of what we've discussed is summarized on this simple tool."

"It's simple," said Harold, looking carefully at the tool.

"Can you see yourself filtering out one of five outgoing emails with it?" I asked.

Harold studied the 1-2-3 diagram and taking a deep breath, nodded, "You know, I really think I can cut outgoing email by 20%. Guess I owe you a cup of coffee after all!"

"Then you'll save roughly 10 days a year. Later, I'll show you how to save an additional 5 days by improving email quality and coaching others. After we take a quick break, we'll dive into the quality and clarity of email. Ready?"

"Yes, sensei," Harold bowed respectfully with a glint in his eye. "Ready, willing, and able."

5

A TALE OF TWO EMAILS

After a quick break for coffee (Harold paid!), we began to explore ways to improve the quality of Harold's email. I handed Harold a printed email.

"I'd like you to read this email and stop when you understand the action required." I took out my stopwatch, "Ready, set, go!"

Harold quickly began reading the email, which was titled *One More Thing*.

....

To: Tiger Team National Distribution List
Cc: Ed Henry, Tyler Banks, Sheila Mehta, Cindy Wu
Attachments: NhddMtgNotes.doc, NatSls07.xls
Subject: One More Thing

Greetings.

I wanted to thank you all for your participation in last week's meetings. It was great seeing you all in sunny Florida. The information that you shared was really helpful and it will help us all to better service our customers in the future. In particular, Brenda's insights into the Cray account were really helpful. Her approach serves as a best practice for all of us. I am including the notes and action items for your review. As luck would have it, I need to ask some of you to do one more thing for me. Unfortunately, we need to take a look at our March numbers. We have been hearing that some of the numbers are being reported incorrectly. Other people are finding that the numbers are fine. If we want to get full credit for everything we do, we should jump on this immediately. In fact, we might also want to take a look at the February numbers to see if they also look right. This only applies to the East coast team. West coast numbers appear to be fine. So, please review the attached documents and let me know if you see any inconsistencies. I am also including some important information from the meeting including Brenda's best practices.

Oh yes, one more thing: We are looking to see if the March widget sales numbers are higher or lower than the February and January widget sales numbers. Generally speaking, they should be higher. If your numbers are lower, please call me at your earliest convenience.

Thanks again for all of your help last week. I think we got a lot accomplished in a very short period of time. Despite a somewhat cramped room and...let's just say, not the best food, we managed to execute like the champions that we are!

Andy

....

As Harold read, he sighed and shifted uncomfortably in his chair. The writer was communicating for a purpose, but the specific action was nowhere to be found.

"*Get to the point!*" Harold muttered impatiently. The message concluded with a vague request to send a report into headquarters. Harold looked up to indicate that at last, he was done. "Phew. I think this message is asking the reader to send in the February and March reports — but only if they see something funny in the numbers?"

"You don't sound very confident. Maybe you should read it again." I grinned, glancing at my stopwatch.

Harold groaned and buried his head in his paws. "Don't make me read it again. My hair hurts!"

"It took you 50 seconds to get through it. How'd that feel?"

"Frustrating," groaned Harold. "I get messages like this all the time — they seem to go on and on. Why can't people just get to the point?"

"We'll talk about that later, but first, read this second email and tell me what action is required." I handed another email to Harold, "Ready, set, go!"

Harold picked up the second email and instantly saw that it was much more structured than the first. The action requested was upfront and the key points in the body were neatly bulleted. By simply reading the title, he immediately understood the required action.

··

Subject: Action: Submit district business plan by 5 PM EST 5/15.
Hey Tiger Team – Great meeting last week!

Action:
Follow guidelines below for business plan submission due 5/15.

Background:
- Remember to use specific and measurable goals.
- If you need to review instructions, go here: *www.mydistrictplan.net.*
- Be sure to stay within budget limits-$100k max. Sorry!

Close:
- Call me with questions and thanks for your help.
- Next meeting is 6/15: We'll discuss business plan implementation.

Thanks!
Angela Stevens
Regional Manager
Now Media
45 Power Team Blvd.
Innovation, CT 06437
203-987-6543
astevens@rm.com

··

"I need to send Angela my district business plan by May 15th."

"Seven seconds!" I announced, showing Harold the stopwatch, "How do the two messages compare?"

"The first message took 43 more seconds to read. Plus, I feel like it short-circuited my brain."

"How many of these long, drawn-out emails do you get a day?"

"At least five," replied Harold, "A couple people on our team think of email as a way to share their life story."

"The first email uses what we call a 'wall of words' style. There are no spaces or bullet points, just words, words, words, as far as your tired eyes can see. Five of these per day add up to 1200 confusing and time-consuming experiences a year. Poor email quality increases processing time and errors while confusing clients, but there is an even greater risk."

Harold looked up. "There is?"

"How do you feel about the person who wrote the long and confusing email?" I asked.

"He's completely wasting my time. He's trying to be nice, but he writes really frustrating email."

"What else?"

Harold thought out loud, "Well, he seems kind of scatterbrained and unprofessional."

"Not exactly the type of person that you'd rush to hire or collaborate with?"

"No," sighed Harold. His face brightened. "But I'd like to work with Angela. She's sharp as a tack and really seems to care about her team."

"What you're saying is that each email we send represents a tiny fraction of a *virtual resume* that we create over time. The clarity of your outgoing email now determines a considerable portion of your professional image. That's an important reason to strive for *absolute clarity* in every email you send."

Harold seemed to be reflecting on all the email he'd sent over the past few years. Perhaps he was thinking, "*Do I send messages like Andy or Angela?*" He looked back and forth between the two emails. "I guess I'd be a little nervous if I got placed on a project with Andy."

"Well, here's a surprise for you," I said with a wink. "Both writers are the same person!"

"What?" exclaimed Harold, studying both emails in disbelief, "No way! This Andy guy is an insufferable gasbag. He drones on and on."

"True. But these messages were written by the same person before and after joining the Hamster Revolution. Here's another twist. That *insufferable gasbag* is me!"

"Huh?" Harold stammered, looking embarrassed as I burst out laughing.

"*I wrote both of those messages at different points in my career!*" I explained with a smile.

"I'm sorry," said Harold, looking flustered. "You're Andy *and* Angela Stevens?"

"Yes. I changed the names to show how the Hamster Revolution can transform the quality of a person's email."

"No way!" exclaimed Harold. "I didn't mean…look, you're not a gasbag."

"Relax, Harold. I *was* a rambling gasbag before I learned how to create crisp, well-structured emails. The quality of my business writing probably improved *more* than 50% after joining the revolution. Now Harold, be honest: How do the emails you write compare to these two? Are you long-winded or clear and concise?"

"I was just wondering the same thing," said Harold sheepishly, "I'm probably somewhere in the middle."

"So, there's room for improvement?" I asked.

"Plenty," agreed Harold.

6

STRATEGY 2: IMPROVE EMAIL QUALITY

"So, let's begin improving the quality and clarity of email," I said, handing Harold another small, laminated card. "This is the A-B-C Email Quality Tool and it's going to change the way you write email."

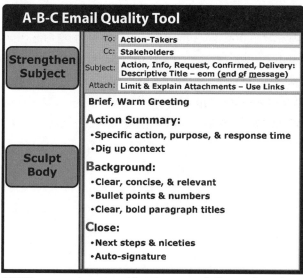

Harold studied the A-B-C tool, "Hey, this is neat. You've put the best practices in the exact place where they'd fall in an actual email."

I grinned, "Right. And we've also chunked the best practices for improving email quality into two important sections: *Strengthen the Subject* and *Sculpt the Body.*" I rose to my feet. "In fact, these two insights are so often overlooked that I'd like you to stand for a special Hamster Revolution memorization ritual."

Harold stood up on his chair with a nervous smile.

Standing tall, I struck the classic bodybuilder's bicep pose. I bent my arms at the elbows and flexed as I said, "From now on, whenever we write an email we must ***strengthen the subject.***"

I then struck another famous bodybuilder pose known as "the crab." This entailed leaning forward and lowering my arms to waist level, making fists and bending my elbows slightly. I flexed with all my might as I turned from left and right, posing for an imaginary audience, "and ***sculpt the body!*** Now you try it, Harold."

"Strengthen the subject and sculpt the body," squeaked Harold, shyly looking around to see if anyone was watching. I got up and closed the door to make Harold feel more comfortable.

"Try it again, but make it louder this time — as if your life depends on it," I insisted with a look of mock exasperation. "Give it some umph, and don't forget to flex!"

This time Harold did the bicep pose and shouted, "***Strengthen the subject!***" He pulled his paws across his small torso in the crab pose, "***Sculpt the body!***" We both laughed at how ridiculous we looked. We repeated the exercise in unison for good measure.

"Good job," I said with a satisfied grin. "From now on you're going to pay special attention to creating emails with ***strong*** subject lines and ***sculpted*** bodies."

"Don't see how I could forget!" smiled Harold sitting down again.

Use Categories to Build Context

"Using simple subject *categories* before your title is a great way to begin strengthening the subject. I recommend using *Action, Info, Request, Confirmed,* and *Delivery.* These categories build context and rapid comprehension for your reader."

Harold nodded, "I'm familiar with *Action, Request,* and *Info,* but when do I use *Confirmed* and *Delivery?*"

"*Confirmed* helps your recipient know that you understand their request and have committed to a particular action. For example, if someone wants to know if you submitted an important proposal to a client, you might respond with an email titled:

Confirmed: Widget Proposal Submitted to Client X on 4/15

Delivery is used when you're responding to a specific request. It's your way of saying, 'I'm delivering exactly what you requested.' This creates instant context for the person who made the original request. For example:

Delivery: Completed Business Plan for Northeast District

"I like that. It leaves no room for misunderstandings," nodded Harold. "Hey, something just occurred to me. I get stressed when I'm unsure if people have actually done what they say they will. I wouldn't have so many nagging doubts if my co-workers used clear categories such as *Confirmed.*"

I smiled at Harold's growing insight, "Isn't it great? Better email yields peace of mind. And teams that use categories get more done because the purpose of each email is easily understood. Another benefit is that recipients can sort their inbox by email category. For example, they can sort their inbox to find all of the *Action* or *Request* emails, which is a great way to streamline workflow and focus on top priorities."

Descriptive Titles Eliminate Uncertainty

"The next key to *strengthening your subject* is to create a descriptive title. Vaguely worded titles are inefficient in two ways: They confuse the reader when they're first received and they also make it harder to relocate an email once it's been stored. Think about finding an email simply titled *Meeting*. How do you know which meeting?"

"Or my personal favorite — the blank subject line," laughed Harold.

"Mine is 'Hi there!' That really makes locating an email easy!" I said with a laugh.

"Unclear subject lines make it tough to find an email that's been filed. So, if you're sending out meeting notes to your team, instead of naming the email *Meeting Notes,* you could title it:

Delivery: Notes from Tiger Team Sales Meeting - 2PM 6/25 Rm. 213

"No confusion there," agreed Harold.

"Using specific dates, times, and places builds context and clarity for recipients. A specific and descriptive title makes email more concise because it forces you to stick with a clearly defined topic."

"Instead of rambling all over the world," moaned Harold.

"A final point on subject lines: Do you know how to *eom?*"

"I'm not really big on meditation," snickered Harold.

I laughed, "*Eom* isn't meditation. It stands for *end of message*. When someone types *eom* at the end of an email title, it means that the whole message is contained in the subject line. This saves time for both the sender and receiver."

"So I don't need to open an *eom* message because the title *is* the actual message?"

"You've got it, Harold."

Use Brief, Warm Greetings

"Before we learn how to sculpt the body of our emails, I thought we should discuss a common concern. Some people like to start off emails with a friendly comment or two to break the ice. Others feel that too much chitchat at the beginning of an email can confuse a message's true purpose. For example, someone may ask how you're doing or what your teammates have been up to lately."

"When the email is really about something completely different," noted Harold.

"Exactly. So, I recommend using a concise salutation such as 'Hi Harold,' plus a *brief but warm* statement at the beginning of my messages. Try to keep the whole greeting to one line with fewer than eight words. Here are a few examples:

Hi Kelly– Nice job on the Baker account.
Hi Mark – Thanks for sending the sales report.
Hey Team – Great meeting last week.

Harold nodded, "These greetings satisfy both the people who want to start an email with a kind word and those who want to get right to the point. It's the best of both worlds."

Use A-B-C to Sculpt the Body

"Now that we've learned how to *strengthen the subject* of your emails, let's look at how you can *sculpt the body* using the A-B-C method. A-B-C is a structure that puts the right information in the right place in the body of every email you send. It increases the *readability* of each message, which helps both the sender and recipient accomplish more. A-B-C can also be used for voice mail, letters, and other communications."

I pointed to the A-B-C tool, "The key is to break the body of your message into three distinct sections:

- **A**ction Summary
- **B**ackground
- **C**lose

Action Summary: An Action Summary is a single sentence that summarizes the specific action, purpose, or key point of your email. Nothing is more frustrating than having to read several paragraphs to understand why a particular email was sent."

"It's really time-consuming," said Harold.

"That's another reason why a powerful Action Summary is becoming more and more critical. A clear Action Summary makes it possible for the reader to quickly respond to an email without having to sift through the entire message or a long email thread. The Action Summary eliminates uncertainty, which allows you to relax your mind and focus on the actions you need to take."

Harold seemed pensive.

"You look thoughtful, Harold. What's up?"

"This is kind of a revelation for me. If all my incoming email became clear and concise, I could focus more on taking action versus figuring out what the other person is trying to convey. I'd accomplish more with a lot less stress."

"Exactly, and for longer emails, the Action Summary is a helpful introduction to the content that will follow. For shorter emails, the Action Summary can be the entire email. In either case, it's important for the Action Summary to provide a healthy dose of clarity and context to the reader."

Dig Up the Context for Short Replies

"In the age of PDAs and text messaging, vague or brief replies are a common cause of confusion. For example, someone might write 'Sounds good.' 'I'm in,' or 'I'm all over it' in response to an email. This kind of reply can cause confusion, especially if the email is a reply to a longer thread in which multiple topics are discussed. In many cases, the short reply is clear to the sender, who knows what he or she's trying to say, but confusing to the recipient. A far better approach is to *dig up* the context of the email thread and jam it into the Action Summary. This saves a great deal of mental energy for the recipient who may be processing 50 or more incoming emails each day. Here are some examples."

Vague Reply	Action Summary Reply
Sounds good.	Agreed: I will shorten the proposal to four pages and add a graph on glazed donut sales by 5 PM 4/15.
I'm in.	Confirmed: I will attend the 4/15 Sales Meeting and yes, I will bring the glazed donuts and coffee.
I'm all over it.	Final Decision: Manufacturing will decrease the production of glazed donuts by 25% starting on 4/15.

Harold nodded, "You're making things absolutely clear right from the start."

"Digging up the context is an easy way to speed communications and improve your professional image. It also increases the odds that people will act on the emails you send."

"This is really helpful," said Harold. He held up a paw as something crossed his mind. "Wait a minute. If our sales team started using action summaries, their emails would be easier to read and understand. Do you think it might impact sales?"

"Absolutely, Harold. Your clients are just as overloaded by email as you. I'm sure they'd appreciate it if your sales team began sending clearer and more easily understood emails. It could definitely increase revenue for Foster and Schrubb. Now let's look at the next section of the A-B-C message structure. **B** stands for Background.

Background section: Here is the body of your message. This is the place where a little sculpting goes a long way. In this section, resist the urge to simply write out all your thoughts in a long, unstructured *wall of words* format. Instead, take a moment to sort and hone your ideas. Then place them in a logical order. Use space to clearly separate one idea from the next, but also try to limit your email to a single screen page. Here are some additional background thoughts:

- **Chunk Your Key Points.** Bullet points are a welcome relief for tired eyes. They're also the easiest way to chunk your key points. If you have more than five sentences in a bullet point section or paragraph, consider creating a bold, underlined heading summary. If you're describing a sequential task or process, use numbers rather than bullets.

- **Define and Limit Attachments.** If your email has attachments, clearly define the purpose of each attachment in the Background section. If you have a long attachment, let the reader know the page and paragraph where the key point can be found. It's a good idea to minimize the total number of attachments you send and to substitute links whenever possible. Links reduce the total number of document versions in circulation while also reducing the amount of data that your IT department needs to back up each day.

- **Keep Emails to Execs Concise.** Executives appreciate crisp communications that get right to the point. Make sure that you aren't including unnecessary and distracting background information when emailing high-level colleagues."

"Some execs tell me that given the sheer volume of email they receive, they're often forced to delete messages that aren't immediately crystal clear," said Harold.

Close section: The end of your email is a great place for:

- **Extensive Niceties.** While it's fine to offer a brief, warm greeting at the outset of your email, it can be distracting when several sentences of chitchat precede an important action request. Placing extended niceties, chitchat, or kudos at the end of your email keeps these sentiments from getting in the way of your core point.

- **Next Steps.** In some emails, it's helpful to provide a description of related events that are likely to happen in the future. These aren't actions but rather general ideas that connect the current email with future initiatives.

- **Auto-signature.** A well-crafted auto-signature provides important contextual information. It identifies who you are and what you do. A strong auto-signature also projects a more professional image while providing alternative ways for people to get in touch with you via phone, IM, fax, or snail mail."

"A-B-C," mused Harold, "Action, Background, Close… that's easy to remember."

"Perfect. Now let's combine our first two Hamster Revolution strategies," I said, handing Harold a 4" x 6" tent card featuring the 1-2-3 and A-B-C tools on the front. "Later, we'll place Strategies 3 and 4 on the back of this card and you'll have one simple desktop aid for the entire Hamster Revolution."

"Cool," murmured Harold as he studied it carefully. "I can put this by my computer and refer to it when I'm processing email."

"And eventually it will become second nature to reduce email quantity while improving email quality."

"And so the revolution spreads," whispered Harold with a wicked grin.

"Any final questions on the quality of email?" I asked.

"How casual should an email be?" Harold asked, "Some people at work seem to be abandoning punctuation and grammar altogether."

I nodded, "It's an outgrowth of our busy schedules and the fact that a lot of people are communicating with PDAs and cell phone text messaging. In your personal life, it's not a big deal to be a bit relaxed with grammar. I don't use the A-B-C structure or get stressed about grammar when I'm letting my mom know how the kids are doing. But at work, email etiquette is important."

"Got it," said Harold. "Any more email etiquette advice?"

"Sure. Here are a few email etiquette best practices to keep in mind:

- ALL CAPS IS CONSIDERED SHOUTING. So is overpunctuating!!!!!

- When you don't use caps appropriate punctuation or proper grammar its a lot harder to understand what ur trying to say.

- Text messaging abbreviations r confusing 2 ur co-workers.

- Avoid using emoticons that others may not understand. ;o)

- Join the AAAAA (American Association Against Acronym Abuse). Explain acronyms before using them.

- Be sure to check your spelling and grammar before sending. Most email programs allow you to do this automatically. Outlook® users can simply hit the F7 key.

- Keep communications clear and concise when messaging to people who speak a different primary language. Also limit use of expressions unique to one culture such as 'We're on a roll!' when addressing a multicultural audience.

"Poor email etiquette screams out me-mail," said Harold, raising his arms high. "Thanks, Coach!"

"You're welcome, Harold. Now that we've covered email quantity and quality, our third and final topic for today is Info-Coaching. Would you like to learn how to get your colleagues to send you clear, concise, and actionable email?"

"And less of it?" asked Harold hopefully.

"Much less," I replied.

"Bring it on," said Harold.

7

STRATEGY 3: INFO-COACHING SUSTAINS RESULTS

Harold leaned forward in his chair. This was the moment he'd been waiting for.

"So what about everyone else?" he asked eagerly, "How do I get *others* to send me better email? How do I get *them* to join the revolution?"

"The key is to become an effective Info-Coach."

"How do I do that? I'm pretty new at this."

"I understand how you feel. After all, Info-Coaching is a new concept. Only 15% of the professionals we surveyed receive regular coaching on information-management related tasks like email. Yet 89% believed that coaching could improve the value of email."[9]

"Why is it so rare?" asked Harold.

"There are actually three interrelated challenges, Harold.

1. **Defensiveness:** Some professionals feel embarrassed or annoyed when coached on a common task like email. Sensing this, many simply refrain from coaching.

2. **Lack of Execution:** When people *do* learn a best practice or guideline, they often fail to implement it for very long because there is no tool or standard to remind them.

3. **Lack of Knowledge:** Without training or experience, professionals have no idea how to provide Info-Coaching.

"So how do you change all that?" asked Harold.

"With this." I handed Harold another small laminated card.

"Let me guess, another tool?" chuckled Harold.

"Right," I smiled. "This is the Hamster Revolution Info-Coaching Tool. It will help you evolve into a successful Info-Coach over the next few weeks. This tool outlines three simple steps you can take to address the three challenges I just mentioned."

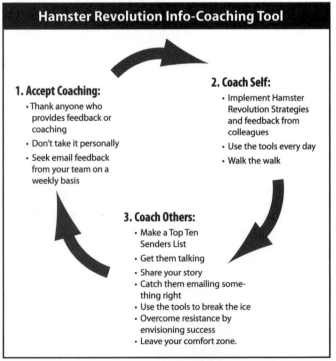

Hamster Revolution Info-Coaching Tool

1. Accept Coaching:
- Thank anyone who provides feedback or coaching
- Don't take it personally
- Seek email feedback from your team on a weekly basis

2. Coach Self:
- Implement Hamster Revolution Strategies and feedback from colleagues
- Use the tools every day
- Walk the walk

3. Coach Others:
- Make a Top Ten Senders List
- Get them talking
- Share your story
- Catch them emailing something right
- Use the tools to break the ice
- Overcome resistance by envisioning success
- Leave your comfort zone.

Harold examined the Info-Coaching Tool. "So first I've got to accept coaching from others?"

"Exactly. It can be frustrating and embarrassing to receive coaching on a common task like email. Instead of becoming defensive, *thank* the person providing the coaching and ask for more feedback."

"It was a bit uncomfortable looking at my email inbox with you today," said Harold.

"But did it help?"

"You bet."

"Being receptive to coaching gives you credibility as you begin to provide it to others."

"I'll definitely start asking for feedback," said Harold glancing down at the Info-Coaching Tool. "And I totally *get* the second Info-Coaching step: Coach Self. *Walking the walk* really makes sense. I've got to implement everything I've learned, so that I can lead by example."

"Right. It's hard to ask others to change when you have not."

"So I combine the 1-2-3 and A-B-C Tool insights with the feedback I get from my colleagues and make sure that I put everything into practice."

"Right. Now you've set the stage for step three, the most rewarding and challenging aspect of Info-Coaching — Coach Others. We're going to spend the rest of our time today discussing this topic. Ready to leave your comfort zone, Harold?"

"Yes, but I'm not exactly sure where to begin."

"Let's start with the results we hope to achieve. Visualize what it would be like if everyone at Foster and Schrubb responded to your incredible Info-Coaching and joined the Hamster Revolution."

Harold leaned back in his chair and put his paws behind his head. He squinted as if he was trying to peer into the future. "The entire company would get a lot more done. Our inboxes wouldn't be overflowing with unnecessary, confusing messages from colleagues. The email that we'd get would be clear, concise, and actionable. I think everyone would feel calmer and more focused."

"Okay, Harold, use that powerful vision to motivate yourself. That's where Info-Coaching can take you."

"It *would* be amazing," mused Harold. "But…"

I raised my eyebrows, "But what?"

"Beyond the concept of Send Less — Get Less, how on earth can I control what other people do with email?"

I looked at Harold's computer again. "Perhaps you have more control than you think. Roughly what percentage of your email comes from people you consider to be *teammates?*"

Harold looked at his inbox. "Well, I'm on a bunch of teams: the HR team, the Organizational Effectiveness team, and several small project teams. It looks like 60% of my email comes from people I consider to be teammates."

"Do you give those people feedback on general business issues?"

Harold nodded, "Of course. We're big on feedback at Foster and Schrubb. It's one of the cornerstones of our leadership model."

"…except when it comes to email?"

Harold was pensive. "I get your point. If most of our email comes from teammates, why shouldn't we provide feedback on that, too?"

"I believe in the 80–20 rule, Harold. I'll bet a large percentage of your email comes from a small subset of people — many of whom are your teammates. We need to target our Info-Coaching to the ones who send us the most. Who are your top ten email senders, Harold?"

Harold shot me a look that said, "*I have no idea.*" I motioned for him to look at his computer. He thought for a moment and then sorted his email inbox by sender. Instantly, he could tell who was sending him the most email. He jotted the names down on a piece of paper.

"Now write one coaching suggestion for each person on your list. Use the 1-2-3 and A-B-C Email Tools as your guide."

Harold reviewed the emails that had recently been sent by his teammates and compiled his list of people and suggestions. When he was done, he slid his list across the desk to me.

"Now you know *who* needs *what* kind of Info-Coaching."

Harold's Top Ten Email Coaching List	
Name	**1 Area of Improvement**
1. Dhara Mehta	FYI emails
2. Roger Fields	Reply-to-all
3. Janet Edwards	Wall of words
4. Mary Wong	Confusing background
5. Enos Knitz	No caps!
6. Marsha Waters	Reply-to-all
7. Sales Team (Dave A.)	Strength subject-ABC
8. Jon Fripp	CYA, FYI, Reply-to-all
9. Carol Schultz	Incomplete PDA emails
10. Ali Nanda	ABC

"But aren't these people going to be defensive like you said?" asked Harold.

"Isn't that true of every kind of coaching, Harold? At first it's awkward, but what's the alternative? Not getting your needs met? Ignoring an efficiency problem? The time for action is now. Email volume is rising at a compounded rate of 14.6% per year."[10]

"Time to leave my comfort zone," said Harold firmly.

"Right. Tell me something, Harold. How do you feel when someone directly states their needs?"

"It's refreshing. I immediately understand how I can help them."

"Can you see the benefit in sharing your email-related needs with colleagues? Wouldn't that be a gift of sorts?"

"It would," said Harold tentatively. "It could help them get more done and improve their professional image."

"Exactly. So tell me about some of the people on your Top Ten Email Senders List?"

Harold nodded, "Okay, let's start with the toughest person on my list: my boss, Dhara Mehta. She's a great leader, but she sends out a ton of FYI emails every day. No one has the time to read them all. Sometimes she loads these emails up with long attachments. I can't just walk in and tell my boss to knock it off."

I thought for a moment. "It can be awkward to coach a supervisor or executive. But in many cases, they and their assistants are the ones sending email to the largest number of people."

"True," agreed Harold.

"What price does Dhara pay for *not* knowing how frustrating her emails can be?"

"Well, she's missing a chance to make us more productive. She's losing a chance to address an issue that's causing frustration for her team." Harold scratched his chin, "Maybe I could share the 1-2-3 and A-B-C tools with her but I'm still a little nervous. After all, she's my boss."

"Hmm," I thought for a moment. "Here's a strategy for the next team meeting attended by Dhara. What if you requested 10 minutes on the agenda for an email efficiency discussion? Show the 1-2-3 and A-B-C Email Tools to the team and explain how it has helped you become more effective. Good leaders like Dhara will often ask if you have any feedback for her. If she does, that may be an opportunity to bring up the FYI light emails. Another option is to discuss it offline."

"Hmmm," said Harold. "She usually does ask for feedback at meetings so that might just work. And my whole team would see this as a way to be more productive."

"Who else is on your Top Ten Email Senders List?"

"Roger Fields reports to me and he's very chatty on email. He hits that *Reply-to-all* more than anyone on our team. I could probably use a more direct approach with him."

I nodded. "I use the direct approach whenever possible. However, I'd recommend first telling him about your experience with the Hamster Revolution and asking for feedback on how you're doing with email. You might learn something about your own messaging habits. Then, in a one-on-one setting, provide him with direct feedback on how *Reply-to-all* impacts productivity. Ask him to consider replying *only* to the primary sender, which in many cases is probably you."

"That might work with Roger, but I'm not so sure about some of HR's internal clients," said Harold. "For example, I've been assigned to service the Sales Management Team and those people are tough. They're a really talented, hard-driving bunch, but they hate spending time on anything that doesn't relate directly to closing business deals."

"What kind of Info-Coaching do they need?" I asked.

"Well, they often send really vague email requests from their wireless PDAs. Their subject lines are often single words such as *meeting* or *FYI*. It leads to a lot of misunderstandings. The sales team is led by a VP named Dave Anderson and we've knocked heads a few times over the years. He's a real driver and a bit defensive."

I thought for a moment,."I always try to keep two things in mind when working with sales teams: (1) They're paid to have a laser-like focus on their clients' needs and (2) They're usually frustrated by administrative burdens that reduce face time with customers."

Harold's face brightened, "So maybe I should frame the discussion around increasing sales and decreasing admin."

"And because you mentioned that Dave is a bit defensive, first explain an email skill that you're working on. Bring the 1-2-3 and A-B-C Email Tools and explain how they've helped you. Defensive people relax when they realize they're not being singled out. Maybe it would help to have a set of tools for each member of the Sales team? You can find them at getcontrol.net"

"Great. I could show how the email tools help everyone create more clear and professional looking email, the kind of email that clients and co-workers really like to get. You know, we've never trained our sales people to create more professional and persuasive looking email."

"…which could ultimately boost sales! We've been helping organizations to do just that. Many sales people needlessly alienate clients with poorly written emails. I have a collection of confusing ones that various vendors have sent over the years. We've contacted many of these companies. Some have asked us to help them create more client-friendly email."

"I hope Foster and Shrubb isn't in your 'collection,'" said Harold, using his paws to make air quotes, "But it wouldn't surprise me if we were. Most of our sales communications flow through email these days."

"And it isn't just Sales that could benefit from improved email skills." I said, "Every team at Foster and Schrubb has its own special reason to join the Hamster Revolution:

- **Information Technology:** IT departments want to reduce email overload so that they can reduce the cost of backing up unnecessary email and attachments. They also field a lot of complaints about email that have more to do with user behavior than with technology problems.

- **Knowledge Management:** Knowledge Management teams are often tasked with improving the net value of information streaming through their organization. Email, the vehicle through which most of our information flows, is a logical place to start.

- **R&D:** Research teams are packed with brilliant scientists and researchers. Although they have great ideas, they often struggle to communicate in a clear and succinct manner. As a result, fantastic ideas are often overlooked or misunderstood.

- **Legal:** Corporate attorneys understand that expensive lawsuits often result from poorly conceived or inappropriate emails. Another legal issue is that lawyers often write long and complex emails that very few recipients understand, which in turn can lead to misunderstandings that result in costly legal proceedings.

- **Project Management:** Colleagues who are responsible for managing critical projects often send and receive an unusually large amount of email. Improving the value of email helps projects stay on track.

- **Executives:** Execs have the challenging task of rolling out major initiatives to large groups of employees. Execution is impossible without clearly communicated plans, action steps, and progress updates. Talented execs often see solid initiatives undermined by poorly written emails."

"And I can certainly see how this will help HR," said Harold. "Almost every day, we communicate important information across the entire organization. If we crafted better emails, I think we'd get a better response and be more valued by the rest of the company."

I nodded, "And Info-Coaching is the key to spreading the Hamster Revolution to all the departments we just discussed. Here's a final Info-Coaching tip. Once you're starting to see results, make sure that you *catch people emailing something right*. For example, you can print out copies of a well-written message and bring it to your next team meeting. Show people what *great* looks like and they'll begin creating great email. You can also include a positive comment in a reply to a well-structured message or discuss email skills at a performance review. If you remain passionate, you will find that Info-Coaching spreads and sustains the Hamster Revolution."

"And in the end, everyone wins," said Harold.

I smiled. "And keep in mind that Info-Coaching is an ongoing process. That's why it's a circular tool. As long as you continually Accept Coaching, Coach Yourself, and Coach Others, you'll find yourself sending *and* receiving less email."

"And the email that I get will be more clear and easier to process," added Harold.

"Exactly."

Harold glanced at his watch and realized that our time was up. "Time to put *Operation Reclaim Harold's Life* into action," he said with confidence. "One small step for the Hamster Revolution — one giant step for me!" Harold packed up his computer and hopped off his chair. Together, we walked to the elevator in the lobby.

"Remember, Harold, change isn't easy for some folks. You're bound to have a few setbacks along the way. We've covered a lot today, but there's more to learn. So feel free to call or IM me whenever you run into trouble. Let's meet at *your* office the same time next week to cover the fourth Hamster Revolution Strategy: effectively filing and finding information. That way, we can see exactly how you're organizing your information."

"I wouldn't call it organizing, more like frantically stuffing email into a bunch of folders or simply letting it accumulate into a mountain in my inbox," said Harold with a grin.

In closing, I asked Harold to complete one homework assignment for me. I wanted him to come up with a rough estimate of how many emails and documents he was storing. As Harold headed out the door, I asked him if the meeting was a good use of his time and if it met his expectations.

Harold reflected for a moment. "Absolutely. I have to admit that it's given me hope. I'm ready to give it a try. Thanks, Coach."

Reader Exercise: Make your own Top Ten Email Senders List. What coaching can you provide? What strengths can you recognize?

List Your Top Ten Email Senders		
Name	**1 Area of Improvement**	**1 Area of Strength**
1.		
2.		
3.		
4.		
5.		
6.		
7.		
8.		
9.		
10.		

8

HELP! IT'S NOT
SO EASY!

Later in the week, Harold pinged me via IM. I was finishing up a meeting with a client.

Harold: Coach, you there?

Info-Coach: Hi. On phone-Give me 2 mins.

Two minutes later...

Info-Coach: Okay, I'm back. Hey – You learned how to IM. Congrats!

Harold: Thanks. I'm waiting for the sales team meeting to start. I didn't want this conversation to be overheard, so I'm using IM.

Info-Coach: I'm impressed, perfect application for IM. What's up?

Harold: This is the HR-Sales meeting. Remember, the sales team sends those vague, confusing emails from their PDAs.

Info-Coach: Yes. I remember.

Harold: I'm a bit nervous. I asked for time on the agenda to discuss email and Dave Anderson was pretty skeptical. He cut the agenda time I reserved down to 5 minutes and said, *"Email isn't a problem here."*

Info-Coach: Okay.

Harold: Well, what if they think my presentation is a waste of time?

Info-Coach: A waste of time? 15 days for you and them? More sales + less admin = more life.

Harold: Yeah, Yeah. I get it. I still don't know how to start. The meeting begins in 3 minutes. They're filing in already. They look grumpy. Maybe they didn't hit their sales quota. I think I'm gonna barf.

Info-Coach: Relax and take a deep breath. Focus. First, get them talking.

Harold: Okay, I'm breathing again... oxygen returning to brain. OK, now what?

Info-Coach: Ask them what bugs them most about email.

Harold: That's it? That's your big advice? How much am I paying you? Ha, ha.

Info-Coach: Just try it. When they start to vent, explain that you've learned a new system that addresses lots of their frustrations. Ask if they'd be interested in seeing it. When they say yes, hand out the 1-2-3 and A-B-C Email Tools. Did you bring them?

Harold: Yes. Okay. Anything else?

Info-Coach: Ask for feedback on your own email first. Show them that you're willing to listen, learn, and improve.

Harold: Great idea. I hope they catch the spirit.

Info-Coach: They will. You can also send them to the getcontrol.net for more info. There are helpful online exercises, efficiency tips, and . . .

Harold: That sounds like shameless self-promotion.

Info-Coach: Perhaps, but the site does have lots of helpful and free info.

Harold: Okay. Gotta go. Meeting starting.

Info-Coach: Call me at 2 PM. I'll keep my phone line open.

Harold: Got it. Out.

Info-Coach: Let them vent. Listen first.

Harold: What part of "Out" don't you understand? Ha, Ha.

At 2 PM the phone rang. It was Harold and he was excited. "It worked! I got them venting and soon everyone was joining in."

"Perfect. What did you cover?"

"There were so many concerns raised. It was really amazing. They have more issues with email than I do. Even Dave had some complaints about angry messaging. He loved the 24-Hour Rule."

"Dave? The guy who almost cut you out of the agenda?"

"Two minutes into the session, everyone was pointing out what frustrated them about email. A couple top sales managers repeatedly mentioned it was reducing face time with clients. Dave loosened up after that."

"Great. Did you ask them for feedback on your email?"

"Didn't have to. They picked apart a few of my recent emails on the spot. To be honest, they were right. The whole HR team tends to be a bit verbose. I showed them the tools and the website. They seemed really interested in learning more about the Hamster Revolution."

"What were the specific outcomes of the meeting?"

"Everyone committed to talking to their people about the Send Less — Get Less principle in order to reduce email volume. The sales managers are going to help their people to *strengthen the subject* and *sculpt the body* of each email they send. They're interested in learning more about Info-Coaching and team training. Dave seemed really pleased with the discussion."

"They got it," I said with relief. "Good job, Harold."

"It was the last thing they wanted to fix and now it's at a top priority," crowed Harold.

"And how do you feel?"

"Great. I feel like we accomplished something important for one of HR's hardest-to-please internal clients, something we should have addressed a long time ago. This brought our teams together to tackle a common enemy and that's a powerful thing."

"Remember to catch Dave and other members of the Sales team *emailing something right* in the next couple of weeks. I'll see you in a few days."

Our next meeting had been strategically scheduled to occur at

9

HAROLD'S PROGRESS CHECK

Harold's office in the Foster and Schrubb HQ building. Janet, Harold's administrative assistant, greeted me with a big smile as I stepped off the elevator. She leaned over and whispered, "So you're the one who's helping Harold with his email?"

"I am," I said with a smile.

"Well, just between you and me, it's working."

"What's working?"

"The Hamster Revolution."

"You know about the Hamster Revolution?"

"Of course! That's all Harold's talked about for the past week."

"Has anything changed as a result?" I asked.

"It's made my job a lot easier. I don't manage Harold's inbox, but we do send each other a lot of email. He's suddenly sending a lot less to everyone and the email he does send is much easier to understand. And one other thing…"

Janet stopped walking and whispered, "He seems a little more like his old self, if you know what I mean."

"In what way?" I asked leaning forward.

"Well you know," said Janet cautiously, "in his overall, er, demeanor."

"Since you brought it up, just how long has Harold been a ham…?"

"Ahem!" We both looked up and saw Harold smiling as he walked down the hall toward us holding two cups of coffee. He was definitely still a hamster, but a happier and more relaxed hamster than when we first met.

"Well here's Mr. Sunshine himself!" laughed Janet nervously.

"Thanks for walking me in, Janet. I'm glad things are going well," I said with a smile.

Harold thanked Janet and handed me a coffee. "Here's my office, Coach," he said, "Come on in."

It was a small, well-furnished office that featured a picturesque view of the city. Harold had a beautiful wooden desk with a few piles of paper on it. His leather chair had a couple of phone books stacked on it so that he could work more comfortably. I noticed that he had placed the email productivity tools right next to his computer.

"Before we talk about how you file and find your information, I'd like to know how things are going with the email insights we discussed last week."

Harold sat down at his desk and motioned for me to take a seat.

"I let everyone know that I'd joined up," he beamed, "and that got a whole bunch of email Info-Coaching conversations rolling. It was tough and a little awkward at first. I really did feel anxious. I simply explained how I was trying to change my email habits and that seemed to interest a lot of people. At first people laughed at the whole hamster thing but then I told them about saving 15 days a year."

"That got their attention?" I interjected.

"It did. My boss Dhara and Janet were a bit defensive at first. I took your advice and asked for feedback on my email. They gave me some great coaching and then allowed me to provide coaching to them. Apparently, some of my emails weren't as clear as I'd originally thought. Dhara's definitely sending fewer of those FYI emails that were slowing me down."

"And you've been following up with other people on your Top Ten Senders List?"

"Yes and I took it one step further. I added a little tag line at the end of my outgoing emails."

"What does it say?" I asked.

"Sick of Email Overload? Join the Revolution! Ask me how."

"Wow. Great idea, Harold."

"And people can't help but ask, 'What in the world are you talking about?'"

"And once the conversation starts…"

"…the revolution spreads!" laughed Harold. "I'm definitely saving more than 30 minutes a day thanks to the Hamster Revolution. That's two and a half hours a week or 15 days a year. It's weird, I'm suddenly able to focus on what matters most without feeling so harried."

"You're making great progress, Harold."

"Thanks, but it gets even better. Kyle and I talked about karate and we're going to build it into our schedule. I'm also starting to put my ideas together for the Accountability Project. It's long overdue."

I smiled and we sat for a moment without talking.

Harold said, "I can't thank you enough, Coach. I've still got a long way to go. But already, I'm a bit of a zealot; I really love sharing the Hamster Revolution strategies with people. I've also come to understand that not everyone will join and that's OK, too."

I smiled, "You've accomplished a great deal. Our work is more than halfway done. Now it's time to focus on the way you file and find your info. Are you ready for the fourth Hamster Revolution Strategy?"

Harold looked nervous but excited. "Sure. But this won't be pretty. My files are a mess."

My files are a mess! I'd heard this confession a thousand times. This

10

CHAOS IN INFO-LAND

was the big, dirty secret of the information age. In fact, 78% of the 2,000+ professionals we'd surveyed reported that they *often* find it time-consuming and frustrating to locate email and documents.[11]

"Harold, has anyone ever helped you organize your files?" I asked.

"Not really. A few colleagues have given some advice, but it hasn't helped. By the way, I completed that homework assignment."

"Great. So how many emails and documents are stored on your computer?"

"Over 8,000!" said Harold, "I'm amazed that I've accumulated so much stuff."

"That's like managing a small town library without any training," I noted. "Mind if I move my chair so I can see your computer screen?"

"Not at all," said Harold.

I picked up my chair and walked around Harold's desk so that we could both look at his computer at the same time. Together we explored the various places where he stored his information.

Harold had email, documents, and links stored in several places:

- Email Inbox: 454 emails.

- Email Storage Folders: 57 primary email folders jammed with over 5,000 emails. A few of the folders had sub-folders, but most were filled with hundreds of emails.

- Document Storage: 45 document folders packed with several thousand documents and attachments.

- Links: 211 links stored in one long list in *My Favorites*.

Harold got up and pointed to his filing cabinet. "And things aren't much better in here. I call this the Blue Monster because it eats up all my hard copy documents."

I stood and walked over to Harold's filing cabinet, which was about 10 feet from his desk. Its four drawers were jammed with over a hundred folders in a rough kind of alphabetical order. Some of the folder names matched his computer files, but many were different. He had used different colored folders and various types of pens and markers for his labels. There was a lot of variation.

"Things just seem to vaporize," said Harold with a vacant look in his eyes. We walked back to our chairs and sat down.

"You're not alone, Harold. Remarkably, half of all initial attempts to locate information are unsuccessful. That's a lot of wasted time and energy. The time spent searching for lost information costs companies like Foster and Schrubb $5,000 per employee each year. For a company like yours with over 8,000 employees, that's $40 million a year in wasted time.[12] Even in this era of powerful desktop search tools, many people feel oddly *disconnected* from their information."

"That's how I feel," stated Harold flatly, "disorganized and disconnected."

"Did you ever wonder why?"

"Why what?"

"Why it's such a struggle to get your arms around your info?"
Harold paused. "I guess I've never really developed a consistent
way of organizing things. I just stick emails into folders and make
up folder titles as I go along. Other times I just let emails pile up in
my inbox. We're so busy these days, going from project to project
with little administrative help. There's no time to get organized." He
paused and then shot me a worried glance, "Why do *you* think I'm
struggling?"

"I find that most professionals focus on *what* they store rather
than *how* it's stored. They end up managing a heap of difficult-to-
locate email and documents. That's inefficient…"

"…and stressful too," added Harold emphatically.

I nodded. "A lot of people that we speak to agree: Organizing
8,000 of anything without guidance and a solid plan doesn't make
much sense, does it?"

Harold shook his head. "I should have taken the time to figure out
a better system."

"I think you've done the best you could. Almost every client I
work with starts from the same place."

"Well it's time for a change," said Harold, "So what's the plan,
Coach?"

I smiled. "Today, you'll discover the most revolutionary aspect
of the Hamster Revolution: a powerful new way to organize your
folders called COTA.® If you like it, we'll begin setting up COTA on
your computer. But first, I'd like to share three challenges with your
current organizational system. I'll also provide ways that you can
address these challenges. Whether or not you adopt COTA, these

insights can help you design a better way to store your info. Sound good?"

"Sure," replied Harold, "Hey Coach, is COTA software?"

"No. It's an easy-to-use folder system. We start with four *primary folders* and then provide you with six storage secrets that make storing and retrieving information easier and more effective."

"What do you mean by *primary folders?*" asked Harold.

"When you go to the place in your computer where you store your documents or email, you'll see an initial list of storage folders that you've created, right? Those are your *primary* folders. Folders placed inside those folders are *sub-folders*. Okay?"

"Got it," said Harold, "So what's wrong with my current system?"

Challenge 1: Overlapping Categories

"First of all, you're using a number of *overlapping* primary folder categories. Have you ever looked for a document on your computer and had to hunt from one folder to the next thinking that it could be here or here or there?"

"All the time!" chuckled Harold. "It's frustrating."

"I know. Let me show you why that happens." I got up and began to write on Harold's whiteboard, "Here are the names of three of your actual email storage folders. I've also included the general categorization method that you use for each one."

"What's wrong with those folders?" asked Harold defensively. "I

Email Folder Name	Categorization Method
Spreadsheets	Filed by Type of Software
Stuff Sent by Boss	Filed by Sender
Training Programs	Filed by Content

learned some of these in my time-management class."

"Individually, these are good folders. But taken together, they overlap and cause confusion. What if your **boss sends** you a **spreadsheet** related to a **training program**? Where do you file that message?"

Harold was about to say something but then he paused and frowned, "Okay, I see — that message could be stored in any one of these three folders. So when I come back to find it, I'll never know exactly where it is."

"And that *uncertainty*, caused by overlap, is the main reason why things are always 'vaporizing' on you. You've created a folder system where overlap is *the rule* rather than the exception. Over time, the *more* you use your folder system, the *harder* it is to find information. As you accumulate more and more stored documents with multiple hiding places, your system falls apart and suddenly you're lost in a vast wasteland of information."

"The harder I work, the harder I have to work," sighed Harold, appearing to sense the connection to his email woes. He was looking at his computer files as if seeing them for the first time. "And info-glut wins again."

"The key is to pick one method for categorizing your information and stick with it. Selecting a single method greatly reduces overlap, decreases uncertainty, and defeats info-glut. We'll look at a great way to do that in just a moment."

"Okay, what else is wrong with my system?" asked Harold eagerly.

Challenge 2: Too Many Primary Folders

"You've created 57 primary email storage folders."

"So?"

"Each time you try to file or find an email, you have to decide between 57 possible email folders. What do you think about that?"

"57 choices, changing all the time," mused Harold. "That does sound a bit complicated."

"A bit?" I asked. "Try *a lot* complicated. If you owned a restaurant, would you list your food in a long alphabetical list of 57 items? No, you'd chunk your menus into three master categories: Breakfast, Lunch, and Dinner. Right?"

"Yes," agreed Harold.

"Now why would you do it that way?"

"So people could easily find what they wanted to order. I get it; it's kind of like the Dewey Decimal System in libraries or the Dairy section in a grocery store."

"Right," I said, "Our brains aren't good at juggling 57 options at one time.[13] It causes stress and fatigue. Unlike your filing system, effective storage systems break items down into logical chunks."

Harold twitched his whiskers thoughtfully as he stared at his computer files. "To find and file information fast, you're saying that I need to reduce the number of primary folders I use."

"Exactly, and that's why it's important to choose five to seven mutually exclusive primary folders that remain consistent over time. Again, you'll learn an easy way to do that in just a moment. But first, let's explore one final issue."

Challenge 3: Mismatched Folder Systems

"Because you create your folders on the fly, over time, all of your different storage areas have evolved *differently*. Your primary email folders are set up differently from your document folders." I pointed at the Blue Monster. "Your filing cabinet contains different folders than your computer folders. That's a problem because…"

"Nothing matches," interrupted Harold staring blankly at his computer screen. He surfed from his email folders over to his document folders. He looked at all the links he had stored in *My Favorites* and glanced over at his filing cabinet. "Everywhere I turn, I see different looking storage systems and I have to shift mental gears to remember how each one works."

"And that makes *multitasking* harder because you're constantly jumping between all of these mismatched storage systems all day long. That's why most people complain about their team's shared drive; it's another place they have to go that doesn't match."

"I despise our team's shared drive. Talk about a black hole…"

I let Harold vent a bit and then continued, "So the final key is to develop one simple folder system and extend it to *all* of the places where you store information. Now let me show you how COTA addresses everything we just discussed."

"Hold it." Harold raised his paw. "I want to learn about COTA, but what about desktop search software? Wouldn't that solve the problems you just mentioned?"

I got up and walked to the window. Turning to Harold, I said, "I like desktop search. But in my opinion, search is only half of the solution. I believe that it's much more important, from a workflow perspective, to actually *know* where your information is located. When you create an effective folder system, navigating to the right information suddenly becomes a breeze. Your information is ordered and accessible at all times. You can zoom in and grab what you need without having to think up keywords that may yield no hits or 1,000 hits. That's why I use desktop search as a complement to my COTA system."

"I guess I was hoping for a silver bullet," mused Harold.

"That's understandable," I said, "Millions of people can't find half of their emails and search can be very helpful. But a well-designed folder system helps you browse for ideas, best practices, and files that you'd never think to search for. It helps you see relationships between seemingly unrelated pieces of information in the electronic *and* hard copy worlds. For me, it's the difference between efficiently *managing knowledge* and endlessly *searching* for things. There's a big difference between knowing and searching. And Harold, we search only for things that are lost to us. But what if your information wasn't *lost* in the first place?"

Harold leaned forward, "Well, *lost* is exactly how I feel when I'm trying to find things these days. I want to learn COTA. I want to be in control of my information, instead of the other way around."

"Then let's go to COTA," I said walking from the window back to my chair.

11

STRATEGY 4: FILE AND FIND IT FAST WITH COTA

"I've helped lots of people organize their email and documents so that they could file and find everything fast. After working with hundreds of people with all different kinds of jobs in all different size companies I began to notice an intriguing pattern."

"What kind of pattern?" asked Harold.

"I started to notice that we were winding up with the same four primary business folders over and over again."

"But what four folders could possibly work for people from 50 different professions?" exclaimed Harold, looking a little nervous. "There can't be a one-size-fits-all solution."

"That's what I thought at first," I said. "It went against the grain of everything I'd been taught about storing information. So I kept trying to ignore the pattern, but it kept repeating."

"What did your clients think?" asked Harold. "Did the system work for them?"

"They were thrilled because the system was easy to use and didn't fall apart over time. At last they felt organized and in control. The quality of their work improved and their careers took off because the new system didn't require a lot of thought or memorization. And because the system was *universal*, they could use it even when they changed jobs."

"Useful," said Harold leaning forward, "No more reinventing the wheel whenever the wind changes direction."

I nodded. "Over the years, I continued to make improvements. I tried each idea on myself first to see if it really worked."

Harold furrowed his brow. "So you eat your own dog food?"

"Excuse me?"

"It's an expression. If you manufacture dog food, someone on your team has to taste it before feeding it to the dogs. Otherwise, how would you know if it really tastes good?"

I laughed. "I get it. And yes, I use COTA. It's on my computer, it's in my filing cabinet, and it's even on my team's shared document area. I eat my own dog food every day and I love it!"

"Good," said Harold looking relieved, "'cause I don't want to be a guinea pig!"

"Understood," I said with a smile.

"So what exactly is COTA?" asked Harold.

"COTA is an acronym for four primary folders that hold all of your business information. Once I describe the system, you'll see how it effectively organizes information while eliminating overlap."

I handed Harold another tent card. "Here's your fourth and final Hamster Revolution Tool. As you can see, I've placed all four

Hamster Revolution Tools onto one simple 4" x 6" card. You can place it by your computer as a constant reminder of everything you've learned."

Harold examined the tool carefully, "Wow, this is handy. But, I'm going to need a little help understanding COTA."

The COTA Tool	
COTA Folder	**Contains Business Info Relating to:**
1. **C**lients	Your team's internal or external clients
2. **O**utput	Your team's products and services
3. **T**eams	Your team
4. **A**dmin	Your non–core-job responsibilities

©2007 getcontrol.net, inc., Inc. All rights reserved. Copy only with permission.

"Learning COTA is a little more involved than everything we've covered so far. So let's do a little exercise that will make it easier for you to understand its power and usefulness. Close your eyes for a second and take a deep breath."

Harold seemed reluctant, but when he saw that I was serious about the exercise, he closed his eyes and took a deep breath. "Okay, Okay. Let the COTA hypnosis begin," he grinned.

"Let's start with the COTA Team folder." I said, "Think back on all of the jobs you've had in the last 10 years."

"Okay," said Harold.

"Have you *ever* had a job where you weren't on some kind of team?"

Harold pondered this simple question, "No. Even when I sold advertising for my college newspaper, I was on a team."

"And so naturally, you had to store information *about* the team that you were on: things such as rosters, business plans, meeting notes, team projects?"

"Of course," smiled Harold with his eyes still closed. "OK, I think I get your point. Because being on a team is a *constant* in the business world, *Teams* is a useful primary folder for storing all information relating to teams."

"Right," I said. "This is the beginning of that pattern I was talking about a moment ago. Let's talk about the *Output* folder now. Were you ever on a business team that *didn't* produce or deliver a product, service, or process of some kind?"

"Never," said Harold firmly, "A business team has to produce something of value. If it doesn't, it won't be around for long."

"Can you give me some examples of the *Output* produced by your current or past teams?" I asked.

"I worked in information technology for awhile and my team's *Output* was customer service for all of our company's computer users. When I worked in advertising sales for my college newspaper, we provided advertising space for local companies. In HR, we *Output* things such as Training Programs, the Benefits Program, and Productivity Programs."

"And you store a lot of information relating to the HR services you just described?"

Harold nodded, "Tons of information."

"So *Output* is also a useful primary folder for storing information, another *constant* as you called it. And if every job you've held has involved a *Team* that delivered *Output* wasn't there always some group of people on the *receiving* end of your *Team's Output*? HR doesn't push its training programs into outer space, does it?"

Harold still had his eyes closed. He seemed very relaxed, "Right. *Outputting* something to no one is futile. In HR, we *Output* our services to the other divisions such as Sales, Finance, and R&D. They're our internal *Clients*."

Harold was silent for a moment. Suddenly he opened his eyes, "Whoa. If *Teams* and *Output* are constants, then *Clients* must also be a constant. *Teams Output* value to *Clients*. That's what business is. That's why COTA worked for all of your clients despite the fact that they were in different industries. It's based on the process of business, which is universal and constant."

Harold eyed the four folders on the COTA tool: *Clients, Output, Teams,* and *Admin*. "I'm starting to get this."

"Do I need to convince you that you also store a great deal of *Admin* info?"

"No," laughed Harold. "*Admin* is inescapable! Your primary COTA folders actually make a lot of sense." He paused and frowned, "but does implementing them really make a huge difference?"

I smiled. "Remember the three challenges we just discussed? COTA has one categorization method: *content*. This eliminates the uncertainty that has caused so much confusion for you. And because COTA uses only four folders, it's easier to zoom to the information you need. You only need to know if you're searching for *Client, Output, Team,* or *Admin* info to start the location process. That's a lot easier than choosing between 57 options."

"Can I use COTA for all the different places I store information?" asked Harold.

"Every single one," I said. "COTA will eliminate the mental friction of multitasking. Whether you're searching for a key email or hard copy document, you have to remember only one simple organizational system: COTA."

"But how long will it take to set up COTA?" asked Harold cautiously.

"About one day."

"I don't know," protested Harold, "I'm awfully busy."

"So far, we both agree that the Hamster Revolution will save you 15 days a year. I'd like you to take one of those days and invest it into setting up COTA. Most COTA users make back their setup time within a couple weeks because suddenly, they can file and find their information in a flash."

"Sounds like a pretty good investment," admitted Harold.

"Do you want to get started?" I asked eagerly.

"One last question," said Harold, pointing at the whiteboard. "Why do you use numbers in front of the COTA folders?"

"When I set up the folders on my clients' computers, the *Admin* folder always came first because computers default to alphabetical order. That seemed wrong to me. I realized that by putting numbers in folder titles we could create a *consistent order* that more closely matches our universal *business priorities*. Over time, I found that it was much easier to work in an environment that reflected my values. So, I placed *Clients* at the top of the COTA order so that I would always be reminded to focus on my client needs. We placed *Admin* in the fourth slot because it's important, but not our top priority."

"Makes sense," said Harold looking nervously at his computer. "So what do we do first?"

Learning COTA: 1. Clients

"Let's start in *My Documents* by creating a new primary folder called *1. Clients*."

"Okay," said Harold as he created the *1. Clients* document folder. He smiled as it moved to the top of his folder list. Harold realized that he had already created folders for most of his internal clients, such as IT and Sales. He simply clicked and dragged the pre-existing folders into the *Clients* folder. We reworked a few things in each folder and deleted a number of outdated documents. In the end, Harold's *Clients* folder looked like this:

1. **Clients**
   - Finance
   - IT Dept.
   - Marketing
   - R&D
   - Sales

"Now you've got all of your client information in one neat place. We'll talk about shaping the middle layers of COTA in a moment. But for now, let's get the four primary COTA folders installed on your computer."

Learning COTA: 2. Output

"Great," said Harold. "I'll bet you want me to create the *2. Output* folder now, right?"

"Right. And these are the products or services your team delivers."

Harold's eyes brightened. "HR *Outputs* a menu of services to our internal clients including Benefits, Recruiting, Productivity Programs, and Training and Development. I have folders for most of those services already."

Harold clicked and dragged a bunch of folders into his *Output* section. He created a couple others and then stopped and frowned, "Here's a problem. This folder is a special productivity project that I did for R&D alone. It could go in either *Output* as a productivity project or *Clients* —R&D. I thought you said that COTA *eliminated* overlap?"

"It does," I said. "We've created a simple rule for this situation. What you've just described is a kind of a tie between two possible COTA storage locations. When you're in this situation, simply use the actual *order of the COTA folders* to break the tie. So a folder that could fit into both *Clients* and *Output* would always go under *Clients* because it comes first in the COTA order.

Harold was thoughtful, "Hey that's actually a good idea because when I'm confronted with another tie and you're not around to coach me, I'll just look at COTA and boom, I'll have my answer."

"Here's another simple COTA rule," I added. "Let's say you're a widget salesperson and you receive a price list containing prices for all 12 kinds of widgets that you sell. Instead of creating a new folder every time you need to store something like this, I would recommend that you use *The General*."

"What general?" asked Harold.

By creating a *General Output* folder, you're strategically creating a place for information that relates to multiple *Output* items. This strategy is also useful if you have a lot of clients."

"So creating *General Clients* and *General Output* folders makes sense because at some point in time, I'll receive information that pertains to all of my clients or all of my output services?" asked Harold.

I nodded. "So the only two COTA rules are: (1) Use the COTA hierarchy to break ties and (2) Use *The General* for documents that pertain to multiple items within a COTA category."

Now Harold's *Output* section looked like this:

2. Output
- Benefits
- General Output
- Productivity Programs
  - Accountability Project
- Recruiting
- Training/Development

"The next COTA category is Teams… right, Coach?"

Learning COTA: 3. Teams

"How many business teams are you on, Harold?" I asked.

"I'm on the Global HR Team and the Organizational Effectiveness Team," replied Harold. As we scanned his folder list, Harold had pre-existing folders for these teams. He created a *3. Teams* primary folder and dragged the pre-existing folders into it. He realized that a number of other sub-folders fit neatly into this section, so he clicked and dragged them as well. His *Teams* section now looked like this:

3. Teams
- Global HR Team
- Org. Effectiveness Team

"And *Admin* is the final primary COTA Folder?" asked Harold, with a growing sense of excitement.

Learning COTA: 4. Admin

I nodded and pointed to the whiteboard. "As we've discussed, *Admin* consists of *non–core-job* tasks… things like your individual compensation information, your…"

Harold rolled his eyes. "This one's easy. Everyone's got *Admin*. Its stuff like expense reports, my computer information, travel information, attendance reports, right?

"Exactly. *Admin* is also your overflow category for that rare file that doesn't fit into the primary COTA folders."

Harold made a *4. Admin* folder and dragged a bunch of his current folders into the COTA structure. Here is what his final *Admin* section looked like:

4. Admin
- Achievement Folder
- Artwork
- Attendance Reports
- Benefits (individual)
- Business Wisdom
- Expense Report
- Forms
- IT and Communications Info
- Policies and Procedures
- Travel
- Vendor Info & Receipts

Harold spent some time surfing through his new COTA folders. He tweaked some titles and created some sub-folders. He still had about 10 remaining folders that didn't seem to fit into the COTA system. Most of them were overlap folders including the *Sent by Boss* folder, the *Urgent* folder, and the *Spreadsheet* folder. Harold took some time and sorted through these folders. He realized that a lot of the content could be deleted or easily transferred into a particular COTA folder.

Harold's COTA folder system now looked like this:

1. Clients
- Finance
- General Clients
- IT Dept.
- Marketing
- R&D
  - R&D Productivity Project
- Sales

2. Output
- Benefits
- General Output
- Productivity Programs
  - Accountability Project
- Recruiting
- Training/Development

3. Teams
- Global HR Team
- Org. Effectiveness Team

4. Admin
- Achievement Folder
- Artwork
- Attendance Reports
- Business Wisdom
- IT & Communications
- Expense Report
- Forms
- Training
- Travel
- Vendor Info & Receipts

"It seems so neat and ordered," said Harold. "So clean."

"Our time is running out, Harold, so I want to give you an important gift." I handed Harold a sheet of paper. "These are the Six Secrets of COTA. Each secret increases the speed and power of the COTA system. Most of the secrets will even help non-COTA users to store information more efficiently. Your homework assignment is to review and implement these Six Secrets over the next week. They're easy to use and you'll be amazed at how they streamline your workflow. If you get stuck, give me a call or visit getcontrol.net for help."

The Six Secrets of COTA*

1. **Use the *Details View* in *My Documents*.** Within *My Documents*, *Details View* allows you to see all documents and folders in a neat vertical layout. It also uses smaller folder icons that make it easier to scan down and find the file you need. Set all Windows *My Documents* folders to *Details View* by going to *My Documents* and selecting *Tools/Folder Options/View/Apply to All Folders*.

2. **Prioritize with numbers.** When confronted by a long list of folders or documents, streamline workflow by adding a number to the title of four or five of the most often used items to bring them to the top of the list.

3. **Use Power Drafts for consistency.** A *Power Draft* is a master folder containing frequently used sub-folders. Copy and rename the *Power Draft* whenever a new folder is needed. For example, you have 20 *Client* folders and sub-folders that all have different names. Unify them over time by creating a standard *Client Folder Power Draft* and copying it whenever you get a new client.

4. **Save time by maximizing access.** Windows users: Maximize access to your information by creating desktop shortcuts to *all four* COTA My Documents folders. Then drag the four shortcuts to your lower horizontal toolbar. (You may have to right-click and unlock the lower toolbar.) This gives you lightning fast access to COTA documents even when you have many other documents open. You can also load the *My Documents* COTA folders into *My Favorites*. Once loaded, you will discover an amazingly fast tool that allows you to zoom in and out of COTA folders without having to open new windows.

5. **Create COTA folders for Net Links.** Many users have hundreds of Internet links but have never created a folder system for them. Create COTA folders for your links in *My Favorites* and you'll be able to manage twice as many links twice as fast.

6. **Convert your filing cabinet to COTA.** Take all of your folders out of your hard-copy filing cabinet and sort them into COTA categories. If possible, use consistent markers, folders, folder-holders, etc. to create a less chaotic view. Try to match the system on your computer as closely as possible and make sure your filing cabinet is within arm's reach of your desk.

Harold read through the list to see if he understood each secret, "Most of these make sense. But I'd like to learn more about *Power Drafts.*"

I nodded. "You have multiple *Client* folders in your primary COTA *Clients* folder, right?"

"Sure," said Harold looking at his internal clients, which included Sales, R&D, and Finance.

"We've discovered that multiple *Client*, *Output*, or *Team* folders often contain the same kinds of information. But because you create them on the fly, all of the folders look different, which slows navigation in the middle layer of COTA."

Harold looked thoughtful. "I know what you mean. I have projects and proposals for all of my clients, but I've named them in many different ways."

"The solution is to create what we call a *Power Draft*. A Power Draft is simply a master folder template with four or five standard sub-folders in a standard order. When you join a new team or take on a new client, you can copy the Power Draft and rename it." I walked to the whiteboard, "Your *Client Power Draft* folder could look like this:

- **ZZ Client Power Draft**
  1. Account Info
  2. Proposals
  3. Projects
  4. PO's
  5. Invoices

"And that way," reasoned Harold, "All my *Client* and *Team* folders would be organized in a consistent way."

"You've got it," I replied, "It's much easier to navigate in familiar surroundings. I usually put a ZZ in front of the title of my Power Drafts so that they slip to bottom of the folder list. That way, I know where to find them."

Harold was getting excited, "Hey! Power Drafting could be really useful for all of the training programs I develop for Foster and Schrubb. Every program has an invitation, a presentation, a workbook. We could create a Power Draft for our team's shared drive. Right now, every training folder looks different. What a mess."

"Your life is getting easier by the minute," I laughed.

As our time drew to a close, Harold showed me a couple of email folders containing several hundred messages that would be very time-consuming to transfer over to COTA. I told him not to worry about transferring all the information. Instead, he could use the folders *as is* for a few months and transfer information over to COTA whenever he encountered something valuable. I told Harold that in my experience, most users find that they can back up and then delete these large email folders after three or four months. In that time, most of the important emails have been opened and saved into COTA during the normal course of business.

"Any final words of wisdom, Coach?" asked Harold as he walked me to the elevator.

"No, but I've got a question for you. What's motivating you to adopt COTA?"

"It seems like my choice is COTA or chaos. I'm sick of chaos. I'll try to implement the Six COTA Secrets this week. I'll also keep using the 1-2-3 and A-B-C Email Tools."

"Fantastic. Where would you like to hold our final wrap-up meeting?"

"How about the same time next week at the Blue Sky Café?" suggested Harold.

"Sounds great," I said as I shook Harold's paw. "See you next week!"

12

A BLUE SKY WRAP UP

Harold and I sat on tall stools at a small table in the Blue Sky Café. This was our final Hamster Revolution meeting and we were toasting Harold's excellent progress. Harold took a celebratory swig from his cup of espresso. Although the cup was small, it seemed rather large in his little paws. The staff, who knew Harold as a regular, seemed nonplussed to be serving coffee to a hamster. But many of the customers stared in disbelief. It was easy to ignore their gawking: After all, we had important things to discuss.

"It's been an amazing week," said Harold. "I converted everything to COTA and I've never been more organized. You were right about email and filing being interrelated."

"How does it feel?" I asked.

Harold paused, "Calm and focused. That's how I feel. On the email side, I'm sending and receiving clear, concise, and necessary messages. Just about everyone's agreed to use the 1-2-3 and A-B-C Email

Tools. And COTA has eliminated a lot of the uncertainty in my life. Now I can quickly find the documents I need to get things done. I'm still learning and I still have some fine-tuning to do, but I finally have a plan that simplifies the management of all my information. It's a huge step forward for me."

"And what about your goals?" I asked.

"Kyle and I found a great karate place and I'm putting together my initial plan for the Accountability project."

Feeling satisfied that Harold was on his way to reclaiming his life, I asked him if he had any final questions or comments.

Harold looked excited. "Coach, I've found some different ways to use COTA."

"You did?" I asked with a smile.

"Yes, I was jotting down my priorities for this week and I spontaneously began sorting my tasks into COTA categories. I was thinking things such as, *Hey, this is an Admin thing that can wait 'til tomorrow but preparing for this Client meeting is absolutely critical.*" COTA seems to make prioritizing easier. Then at yesterday's HR Team meeting we talked about how one of our internal clients wasn't very happy with a training program we delivered. And I found myself talking about how we needed to make sure our *Output* is always in line with what the *Client* needs. Every day I find that I'm using COTA for a lot of different things."

"That's because COTA mirrors the natural flow of business," I said, taking out a pen and sketching a little flowchart on a napkin. "Like we discussed: *Teams* Deliver *Output* to *Clients*. Good clients return value by paying, praising, or supporting your team. *Admin* is a natural by-product of this simple process. One key is that *Admin* shouldn't come between a *Team* and its *Clients*. This process will exist in every job you'll ever hold."

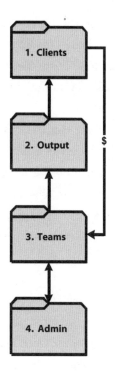

"So naturally, COTA has other uses," said Harold.

I nodded. "Any other COTA stories to share?" I asked. "I love hearing them."

"Yes. Janet, my administrative assistant, really likes COTA. I showed it to her and she agreed to give it a try. I was traveling one day last week and she was able to find several documents in my filing cabinet while I was gone."

"In the Blue Monster?" I asked.

"Now that it's organized by COTA, it has morphed back into a filing cabinet," laughed Harold. "The important thing was that Janet was able to find the right information to help an internal client with an urgent problem. In the past, she wouldn't even have tried."

"That's just the tip of the iceberg in terms of how your team can become more efficient with COTA. Remember, COTA is flexible. If some team members want to use a variation of COTA, that's Okay. But it is nice to have a common way to view information. Wait until you reorganize that shared drive."

"I can't wait," agreed Harold. He shifted on his stool and took another sip of his espresso. "Let me ask you another question," he said. "I have a couple teammates who are interested in COTA. But something is causing them to hold off. One colleague is a manager who considers his boss to be his primary client. Another is a manager who considers the people who report to her to be her clients. This made COTA kind of confusing because these folks regard members of their own teams as clients."

"I would simply explain that designating your team's *real world* clients as *Clients* within COTA is the most practical way to use COTA. This shouldn't diminish anyone's passion for providing excellent service to teammates. However, the COTA hierarchy is a helpful way to visualize your team's role in a broader context."

"That ties into my Accountability Project," said Harold. "Right now, we're seeing productivity decline along with internal client satisfaction levels. Some departments aren't helping others as much as they could. Eventually it trickles down to the service we give our real clients."

"It's a universal business challenge," I said.

"But like you just said, COTA keeps teams focused on their clients," Harold reasoned. "I see it in myself. Over the past week, I've begun to pay more attention to the *Output* that I'm delivering to my internal *Clients*."

"And, if everyone in HR adopts COTA, your entire team will be more client-focused," I suggested. "And as a result, your clients will return more value to your team. This can impact staffing needs, funding requests, and the overall vitality of your team, division, and entire organization."

We sat for a moment quietly sipping our coffee. Then I decided to change the topic. "Harold, what happens to an employee's information when they leave Foster and Schrubb?"

"We just scrub that information off the outgoing person's hard drive and give their computer to someone else. We try to have them download important things that the new person needs, but that rarely happens."

"So all that stored information and knowledge disappears?

"Yup," sighed Harold.

"Ideas, plans, and projects go up in a puff of smoke. This may sound a bit dramatic, but it sounds like a significant portion of your company's knowledge sits on *death row*, waiting for someone to get promoted or retire."

"Or get fired," added Harold.

"And when they're gone, their stored knowledge dies."

"Unless they take it with them to a competitor," groaned Harold. "Then it doesn't die. It comes back to haunt us. We've already lost a lot of business that way."

"You have?"

Harold nodded. "And after someone leaves, the new person comes in and struggles for three or four months trying to find the information and perspective they need to get the job done."

Harold paused, deep in thought. Suddenly, he sat up straight.

"But if everyone knew COTA, it would be different. We could develop a process for transferring the information between outgoing and incoming colleagues. People would be able to see who their clients really are. They would have a kind of contextual compass that would allow them to explore all that accumulated information more efficiently."

Harold was excited by his vision of a more efficient Foster and Schrubb, "Actually, wider adoption of all four Hamster Revolution strategies could have a huge impact on our bottom line," he said, seeing the possibilities.

I felt energized and excited for Harold. Our time was coming to a close and Harold seemed so different from when we first met. "You've done an amazing job, Harold. This is the beginning of an incredible journey for you. Could you sum up your experience over the last few weeks? What are the most important things you've learned?"

Harold thought for a moment and smiled. "When it comes to battling info-glut, I've learned that using the Hamster Revolution strategies is the best *investment* you can make. If you apply the tools and work hard, you can restore order and balance to your life. As far as spreading the revolution goes, start by coaching one teammate, get them excited, and then move on to the next one. If you can help an entire team start a conversation around email challenges, you're halfway home. Share your experiences and shortcomings and connect them to Hamster Revolution insights. Catch everyone emailing something right and a small grassroots movement will emerge."

I remained silent, hoping that Harold would continue. After a thoughtful pause, he said, "When it comes to being an Info-Coach, *walking the walk* is critical. You've got to eat your own dog food or people won't listen to a word you say. You have to leave your comfort zone but it's worth it. When people complain about email, turn their frustration into motivation by giving them effective tools and helping them see the big picture. Email really does add up."

I smiled at Harold's insight. He tilted his head back and thought some more. "Study info-glut," he said slowly. "Find out where it's slowing you down and take action. It's a resourceful enemy that stands between you and your lifetime goals. You can't unlock your fullest potential when you're drowning in email. You can't be a confident leader if you're constantly struggling to find things. These days, you have to have the right information at the right time if you want to win."

"And finally," said Harold as we settled our bill, "I've learned that you have to keep your eyes on the prize."

"What does that mean for you?" I asked as I took the last satisfying sip of my mochaccino, the sip that's got all the chocolate at the bottom.

"Right now it means spending that father-son time with Kyle, being there for him, helping him through this tough patch he's in." Harold's voice wavered and he took a deep breath, "And at work, it means completing the Accountability Project without falling behind. If I can do that, the revolution is a success and my life is back on track."

I was very impressed with Harold's summary. He had absorbed a great deal in a very short time. "You've made amazing progress, Harold," I said as we walked out onto a sunny city sidewalk.

"Coach," said Harold, turning to face me and extending his paw. "Thanks for all the insight, support, and encouragement."

"Good-bye, Harold," I said. "Remember, I'm here when you need me. I've really enjoyed working with you."

"And I, you."

Harold turned and strode confidently down the busy sidewalk. Pedestrians turned in amazement as he walked by. Harold didn't seem to notice. As he rounded the corner he glanced back and raised a fisted paw in the air. It was a sign of determination and purpose. I raised my fist in the air in a show of solidarity and just like that — Harold was gone.

EPILOGUE

"Hey!"

I looked up from my computer screen and was startled to see a stranger's head poking into my office.

"I was just passing by and I thought I'd say hello."

"I'm sorry," I said, "Do... do we know each other?"

"Know each other? Coach, you practically turned my whole life around!"

Then it hit me. "Harold?"

"Well, who else could it be? C'mon, Coach, it's only been six months since our last face-to-face meeting."

"Oh! Of course! Come on in, Harold."

Harold strode into my office and I was amazed to see the transformation. He was an energetic, 35-year-old man with intense brown eyes. He wore a dark blue business suit and carried a sharp looking black leather briefcase. And there was something else... he looked confident and relaxed. Harold looked me right in the eyes as we shook hands.

"I just wanted to stop by to thank you, Coach. Everything you taught me about email and COTA has made a huge difference in my life. Carol and I have never been happier."

"And Kyle?" I asked.

"Check this out," Harold flipped open his PDA and showed me a picture of Kyle and him at karate class, "We're both green belts!"

"And the Accountability Project?" I asked.

"Our leadership team put it on the fast track. It's been rolled out to everyone at Foster and Schrubb; 5,000 people have learned how to take ownership of their team's mission. Internal and external client service ratings are way up — profits, too. The execs are thrilled."

"Excellent," I said as I stood up.

My next meeting was about to start, so I walked Harold out to our lobby and wished him well. As the elevator door opened, we were surprised to see a flustered-looking female hamster step out. She was dressed in a sharp gray business suit and carrying a maroon briefcase.

"Excuse me," she said, as Harold stepped into the elevator.

"Can you tell me where I can find the Info-Coach?"

"I'm the Info-Coach," I said, extending my hand. "Pleased to meet you."

"I'm Iris and this is embarrassing to admit, but I've got a real problem with email. I need help!"

Harold and I exchanged a silent smile as the elevator door slowly closed.

"My job is to help professionals manage their email *before* it manages them, Iris."

"Well maybe I'm in the right place after all," she sighed as we walked down the hall toward my office.

"Say, Iris, do you like coffee?" I asked.

"I'm practically addicted," she replied.

Revolution was in the air.

APPENDIX 1:

FAST ANSWERS FOR BUSY HAMSTERS

Over the next few months, Harold called several times to ask questions. What follows is a summary of those brief conversations.

Harold: Are there any email technology tips I could use to be more productive?

Info-Coach: Absolutely. We've created a free Top Tech Tips Newsletter that you can subscribe to on getcontrol.net

Harold: Should I answer email on the fly or block out time?

Info-Coach: I recommend blocking out 30-minute periods in advance. You can process email more rapidly in *batches* because you can give it your undivided attention.

I also recommend disconnecting your ding — the sound or visual image your computer makes when an email arrives. Most of the time, you don't need to be notified every time an email comes in. If you keep your ding on, it's like planning 40–50 interruptions into every business day. On average, it takes over a minute to regain refocus after being distracted by an incoming email.[14] These distractions sap your energy and slow you down. Another way to limit email interruption is to set your email to synchronize every 30 minutes instead of every 2 or 3 minutes. We show you how on get.control.net

Harold: I ran into several people with email inboxes containing over a thousand emails. Any advice for these folks?"

Info-Coach: Because critical actions and information can be buried in an inbox jammed with thousands of emails, I recommend blocking off a half day and sorting the inbox in a number of different ways to rapidly reduce the number. First, *Sort by date* and delete as many outdated and irrelevant emails as possible. Next, *Sort by sender*. In many cases, you'll often find that a particular sender's email has lost relevance to what you're doing and can all be deleted at once. Next, *Sort by subject* and look for email categories such as *Action, Request, Delivery,* or *Confirmation* emails. These signify important emails that may need to be saved or reviewed before deletion.

Finally, you can sort your inbox by document size. This will bring up emails with large and potentially important attachments. After three hours you'll find that you have significantly reduced the number of emails in your inbox. Make sure you keep track of the opportunities you unearth as you address your backlog. You'll be amazed at the gems that are buried at the bottom of your email inbox ocean. You may need to repeat the process, but it's worth your time and attention. After deleting useless information, spend time aggressively saving important emails and attachments with clear future value.

Harold: Is Hamster Revolution team training available?

Info-Coach: Yes. You can learn about live and virtual Hamster Revolution training at getcontrol.net

Harold: Should I strive to have zero messages in my inbox?

Info-Coach: No, but I do recommend choosing a concrete goal for the optimal number of emails you would like to have in your inbox at any one time. Like it or not, we all use our inbox as a secondary task list. If you have 30 or 40 emails in your inbox, you can actually glance through them pretty quickly and see what needs to be done. I arbitrarily chose 42 as my target number.

Harold: Any tips for deleting or storing incoming email?

Info-Coach: My motto is *Store Less — Find More*. Aggressively delete any message that has limited *future value*. If you can't see a clear purpose for the email, ditch it. Also, if the content of a particular email can be easily found by searching online, on the intranet, or rapidly delivered from another source, such as a co-worker, you don't need to save it.

Harold: Can you show me how COTA might work for some different professions?

Info-Coach: Here's a grid that gives a general idea of how COTA works for different jobs.

COTA Category			
Job Type	**1. Clients**	**2. Output**	**3. Teams**	**4. Admin**

Job Type	1. Clients	2. Output	3. Teams	4. Admin
Sales	External customers who buy or influence what you sell	Actual products, services, and value-added items sold or offered to clients	Teams to which you belong. For example, District Sales Team, Regional Sales Team, Networking Associations, etc.	Benefits Company car Travel Finances Forms Corporate PR Expense Report
HR	Internal customers including IT, Sales, R&D, etc.	Hiring services Benefits package Payroll, etc. Associations	HR team and sub-teams Cross-functional teams Learning and dev. Compliance	All of the above
Doctor	Patients and other institutions that directly control access to patients. For example, hospitals or HMOs.	Healthcare info and other kinds of services related to the health of patients. For example, how to set a broken bone	Office team Associations Hospital Committee Local Medical Group	All of the above
IT	Internal customers including HR, Sales, R&D, etc.	Information related to the IT services and equipment you provide.	IT team and sub-teams Cross-functional teams Associations	All of the above
R&D	Potential consumers	Company's products and value-added products Research data Product development data	R&D team and sub-teams Associations	All of the above

Harold: COTA is for business info. What about my personal info?
Info-Coach: Inevitably, you will store some personal information on your business computer. For now, I would recommend creating a fifth primary folder and labeling it *5. Personal.* We've also created a powerful system for managing personal information called PAO. You can learn more about PAO on www.getcontrol.net/eprod.htm.

Harold: I store half of my info in email folders and the other in My Documents. Isn't it confusing to store things in two places?

Info-Coach: It is. I prefer to store as much as possible in My Documents. Compared to email folder systems, My Documents is much more powerful and simple to use. I find it easier to create, copy, view, and move things in My Documents. Another benefit is that anytime you need to save, insert, browse, or open a document, Windows defaults to the My Documents view and boom... there are my COTA folders and documents. This really pays off when I am inserting things into emails.

Here's a neat trick: from within any Microsoft document, simply hit the f12 key. This allows you to save directly to your COTA system within My Documents. This works for Word, Excel, PowerPoint, and even Outlook emails. If you save both emails and documents into a single powerful document management system, you've got one-stop shopping for all your info. Two words of caution: First, many organizations need to keep email in email folders for legal or security reasons. Be sure to get approval from your IT folks before saving email into My Documents. If they say, "no", you can always use COTA within your email folders. Finally, we just don't know how technology will change down the road so it's impossible to guarantee that email saved into My Documents will be always be recoverable.

APPENDIX 2:

CASE STUDY: CAPITAL ONE'S EMAIL EFFICIENCY SOLUTION

This case study underscores the value of implementing Hamster Revolution insights across a large organization. This case study can also be found at get.control.net

A. SUMMARY

Challenge: Capital One is an organization that constantly strives to maximize productivity. When internal surveys revealed that email overload was a growing productivity challenge, Capital One's Productivity Team took action.

Solution: The Capital One Productivity Team partnered with Mike Song and Tim Burress from getcontrol.net to develop a groundbreaking email efficiency workshop. The Capital One Productivity Team played a major role in shaping the program. The workshop contained insights and exercises found in *The Hamster*

Revolution and other getcontrol.net seminars. Over 2,000 Capital One associates participated in this extremely successful learning and development experience.

B. SITUATION

Capital One (COF) has earned a sterling reputation for innovation, customer service, and leadership in the diversified financial services sector. Capital One manages $103 billion in assets for over 50 million customers worldwide.

In response to internal surveys, Capital One's Productivity Team isolated email as a major opportunity to increase productivity. Associates reported that email was consuming more than 30% of their work day. Internal surveys reflected growing concerns relating to the quality and quantity of email.

C. APPROACH

Capital One's Productivity Team, led by Matt Koch, Director of Productivity and Knowledge Management, made the bold decision to design an email productivity training solution with the following principles in mind:

- **Grounded by data:** Partnering with getcontrol.net, Capital One gathered as much information as possible via focus groups, surveys, external research, etc.
- **Customize and target solution:** The workshop objectives were carefully tailored to reflect the exact needs of Capital One associates. Capital One survey data was incorporated into the workshop to gain added buy-in from participants.
- **Fit the solution to the culture**: Capital One has a corporate culture that expects excellence while always doing the right thing by the customer, the associate, and the company. The workshop was designed to resonate with these core values.

- **Apply intellectual rigor:** Actual results were measured carefully against workshop goals and a pre-intervention baseline survey to validate participants' 75-minute time investment in the email productivity workshop. 2000 surveys containing over 100,000 individual question responses were collected and analyzed.

D. WORKSHOP CONTENT

The powerful email efficiency workshop developed by Capital One and getcontrol.net contained a series of engaging exercises, best practices, and tools that helped participants improve the overall value of email. Some of the elements of the program included:

- Discussion of email challenges
- Review of survey data
- The 1-2-3 and A-B-C Email Productivity Tools
- Exercises that contrasted good and poor emails
- Calculation exercises
- Role plays that helped participants gain Info-Coaching experience
- Written commitments to change behavior

In most cases, participants attended with their teams. This created a lively environment in which team members could discuss ongoing email concerns while creating powerful new team email strategies. Many coaching conversations took place during the seminars. Associates learned:

- How to send fewer email messages
- How to create clear, concise, and actionable email
- How to coach others to become more proficient at email

E. RESULTS

Two months after training, a follow-up survey revealed that:

- **Email decreased by 21%.** Associates reported a 21% reduction in total email sent. There was also a 10% reduction in email received, which demonstrates that the *Send Less — Get Less* concept works in the real world. Participants also reported a 23% drop in the time they spent processing email.
- **Email quality improved by 51%.** Associates reported an impressive 51% increase in email quality over baseline. Clear, concise, and actionable email naturally helps associates accomplish more in less time.
- **11.3 days saved.** Associates reported that they were on track to save 11.3 days per year on average. This figure did not take into account dramatic improvements in email quality, which are likely to have further decreased email processing time.
- **Leadership gains.** The workshop helped to empower associates to take control of the email environment via Info-Coaching. 60 days after training, the percentage of associates comfortable with email coaching rose from 47% to 75%.
- **One year post-training survey metrics.** Capital One and getcontrol.net conducted a One-Year Post Training Survey to determine if results could be sustained over time. The findings were extremely positive:
  - 88% continued to leverage workshop best practices.
  - 83% would recommend the workshop to *all* associates.
  - 80% believed that the workshop made them more productive.
  - 77% indicated that they continued to apply coaching principles gained in the workshop.

F. CONCLUSION

The Capital One Productivity Team did an excellent job of diagnosing and addressing a growing productivity challenge: email overload. They partnered with getcontrol.net *www.getcontrol.net* to develop a highly effective, breakthrough learning experience that resulted in major time savings, improved productivity, and a better work/life balance for associates. Results were sustained over one full year.

Notes

1   Song, Michael and Burress, Tim "Info-Glut and the K-Worker,"
    getcontrol.net White Paper, 2005.

2   Feldman, Susan "The High Cost of Not Finding Information," *KM
    World*, vol. 13, issue 3, 2004, available at www.KMWorld.com.

3   Hallerman, David, "2004 Email Marketing Report," eMarketer.com,
    2004.

4   Song, Michael and Burress, Tim "Info-Glut and the K-Worker,"
    getcontrol.net White Paper, 2005.

5   Cavanagh, Christina *Managing Your E-mail: Thinking Outside the
    Inbox*, John Wiley and Sons, 2003, p. 159.

6   Song, Michael and Burress, Tim "Info-Glut and the K-Worker,"
    getcontrol.net White Paper, 2005.

7   Song, Michael and Burress, Tim "Info-Glut and the K-Worker,"
    getcontrol.net White Paper, 2005.

8   Leland, Karen, and Bailey, Keith *Customer Service for Dummies*,
    IDG Books, 1999, excerpted from "Like it or Not, Voice-Mail Is
    Here to Stay," Sterling Consulting Group, 2004 Press Release.

9   Song, Michael and Burress, Tim "Info-Glut and the K-Worker,"
    getcontrol.net White Paper, 2005.

10 Hallerman, David "2004 Email Marketing Report," eMarketer.com,
    2004.

11 Song, Michael and Burress, Tim "Info-Glut and the K-Worker,"
    getcontrol.net White Paper, 2005.

12 Feldman, Susan "The High Cost of Not Finding Information," *KM
    World*, vol. 13, issue 3, 2004, available at www.KMWorld.com.

13 Miller, George "The Magical Number Seven," *The Psychological
    Review,* vol. 63, 1956, pp. 81–97.

14 Jackson, Thomas Dawson, Ray and Wilson, Darren (Danwood
    Group/Loughborough University), "Evaluating the Effect of
    Email Interruptions within the Workplace," presented at EASE
    Conference (Evaluation and Assessment in Software Engineering),
    Keele University, 2002.

Acknowledgements

The authors would like to acknowledge and praise the incredible contributions of all the brilliant people who helped create this book:

Matt Koch of the Capital One Productivity Team: Your leadership and insight have been invaluable. Thanks for giving us the privilege of collaborating with you and 2,000 Capital One Associates on a groundbreaking knowledge management project.

Elena Song: Thanks for giving us your time and talent, even though you had screenwriting deadlines for Disney, DreamWorks, and Paramount. Your amazing editing, nonstop creative ideas, and ability to keep a straight face while discussing business hamsters helped bring Harold to life.

Bill Kirwin from Gartner: Thanks for being a trusted friend and long-time mentor. Your wisdom flows through everything we do.

Ken Blanchard and Marcus Buckingham: We've learned so much from you over the years. Thanks for lending your voices to The Hamster Revolution. We're deeply honored!

Steve Piersanti from BK publishing: Your brilliant advice reshaped our ideas and helped us create a more reader-centric book. Thanks for your honesty and insight.

Scott Blanchard, Madeleine Homan, Linda Miller, and James Flaherty; Thanks for being wise coaches who've taught us how to help people feel perfect as they act on their best intentions and step into their power.

Mark Forsyth, Margie Blanchard, and Debbie Blanchard from The Ken Blanchard Companies: Thanks for opening doors that we never could have opened ourselves. Your vision and support are greatly appreciated.

Steve Stone and the Infoflows Team: Thanks for building our understanding of software and technology. We can't thank you enough.

Ric Torres of Best Practices: Your business acumen is off the charts! Thanks for the excellent advice, practical ideas, and relentless support.

The authors would also like to thank these fabulous friends and family members who helped us realize a dream:

The entire Song, Halsey, and Burress families, Nicholas and Jake Halsey, Elaine, Jeff, Rox, Jordan and Kendra White, Mary Duncan, Martha Lawrence, Jeevan Sivasubramaniam, Mike Crowley, Pat Zigarmi, Kathy Cuff, Lisa Smedley, Kate Orf, Rubin Rodriguez, Dan Glaser, Nancy Jordan, Charlotte Jordan, Kevin Small, Richard Andrews, Christina Cavanaugh (author of the wonderful *Managing Your Email*), Tom and Nancy Patton, Pam Wiggins, Doug and Cindy Cole, Sean Dailey, Marilyn Kirwin, David Silver, Tom McKee, Steven Covey, Ellen Song, Al and Mary Song, Oreann "Mamaw" Miller, Vic Miller, Garrett Miller, Adam and Michelle Raiti, Doug and Marcia Fazzina, Tony Sheehan, Megan Kahn, Scott Schoenborn, Tim Reichert, Chris Ogle, Chris Dormer, Cory Brouer, Dave and Bridget O'Connor, Lisa Lelas, Patti Danos, Lisa Hiott, John Ireland, Nic Oatridge, Liz Kearns, Jeff and Allison Burress, and info-hamsters everywhere.

Index

SERVICES AVAILABLE

Authors Mike Song and Tim Burress are co-founders of getcontrol.net. They provide *Get Control!* productivity training, speaking and consulting to over 20% of the Global 1,000. Much of The Hamster Revolution is based on *Get Control!* training programs.

Get Control!™ Seminars
Get Control and Get More Done
Save 15 Days a Year!

Get Control! of Email™
Get Control! of Info™
Get Control! of Meetings™
Get Control!™ of BlackBerry®
Get Control!™ of Outlook®

Available in Live Webinar, and e-Learning Formats
Individual, Team, and Organization-Wide Options

Contact getcontrol.net and Receive
a Free Email Efficiency Lesson
1-888-340-3598
www.getcontrol.net   info@getcontrol.net

SERVICES AVAILABLE

The Ken Blanchard Companies® is a global leader in workplace learning, productivity, performance, and leadership effectiveness that is best known for its Situational Leadership® II program—the most widely taught leadership model in the world. Because of its ablility to help people excel as self-leaders and as leaders of others, SL®II is embraced by Fortune 500 companies as well as mid-to small-size businesses, governments, and educational and non-profit organizations.

Blanchard® programs—which are based on the belief that people are the key to accomplishing strategic objectives and driving business results—develop excellence in leadership, teams, customer loyalty, change management, and performance improvement. The company's continual research points to best practices for workplace improvement while its world-class trainers and coaches drive organizational and behavioral change at all levels and help people make the shift from learning to doing.

Blanchard's leadership principles are taught through interactive programs that combine 360-degree assessments, situational case studies, peer feedback, and alignment with core business objectives. Many Blanchard programs blend the use of e-learning with instructor-led training.

Leadership experts from The Ken Blanchard Companies are available for workshops, consulting, as well as keynote addresses on organizational development, workplace performance, and business trends.

Global Headquarters
The Ken Blanchard Companies
125 State Place
Escondido, CA 92029
www.kenblanchard.com
+1.800.728.6000 from the U.S.
+1.760.489.5005 from anywhere

About the Authors

Mike Song

Mike Song is one of America's leading experts on email efficiency and etiquette. A sought-after corporate trainer and keynote speaker, he's helped more than 5,000 professionals take back their lives by managing email more effectively. Mike's speaking and training engagements combine hard-hitting research, humorous stories, and hundreds of best practices to produce results. An ardent researcher, Mike has spent over five years amassing and analyzing data from more than 7,500 workplace surveys on email, information storage, and business meetings. He is co-founder and CEO of Cohesive Knowledge Solutions. Among Mike's clients are such industry leaders as Allianz, Clear Channel, Merck, Fox, HP, and Nestle. Mike lives in Guilford, Connecticut, with his wife Kristin and three children, Emily, Evan, and Ethan. You can reach Mike at *ms@getcontrol.net*.

Vicki Halsey, Ph.D.

Vicki Halsey is the Vice President of Applied Learning for The Ken Blanchard Companies. She is a valued presenter, keynote speaker, consultant, coach, author, and trainer, who also teaches in the MSEL program at University of San Diego. Vicki's expertise in optimal learning strategies, leadership, and blended solutions combine together as she designs and delivers innovative, high-impact leadership, and team and customer service programs. Her passion is helping professionals regain balance and meaning in their lives, so that they return home from work happy and ready to enrich the lives of their families. A partial list of Vicki's clients include: Nike, Oracle, ADP, KPMG, Nokia, Toyota, NBA, Pfizer, GAP, Merrill Lynch, Wells Fargo, Gillette, and Procter & Gamble. Vicki lives in San Diego with her two sons and husband/author, Rick. She can be contacted at *Vicki.halsey@kenblanchard.com.*

Timothy Burress

Tim Burress is the President and Sr. VP of Training for getcontrol. net. He is a talented keynote speaker and trainer. Tim has a 20-year record of excellence in sales, marketing, and training design and delivery. Before co-founding getcontrol.net in 2003, Tim was a Director of Learning and Development at Pfizer. Over the past ten years, Tim has helped over 12,000 professionals manage their information more efficiently. Tim co-developed the acclaimed Info-Excellence Seminar series, which helps teams overcome info-glut and manage information more efficiently. Tim has provided training for: Capital One, Procter & Gamble, Centex, Progressive, and Pfizer. Tim lives in Richmond Virginia with his wife Daphne and daughters Grace and Ava. Contact Tim at *tb@getcontrol.net.*

VISIT
GETCONTROL.NET
AND GROW!

Meet Harold and continue your journey to stress-free productivity at getcontrol.net.

- Free Tech Tips, Exercises, and Newsletters.
- Hamster Revolution Productivity Tools.
- Free Hamster Revolution Discovery Center.
- Training, Speakers, and Research.
- Authors' Blog and More!
- Send a Friend or Your Entire Team!

Visit www.getcontrol.net today and receive a FREE email efficiency lesson.

About Berrett-Koehler Publishers

Berrett-Koehler is an independent publisher dedicated to an ambitious mission: Creating a World That Works for All.

We believe that to truly create a better world, action is needed at all levels—individual, organizational, and societal. At the individual level, our publications help people align their lives with their values and with their aspirations for a better world. At the organizational level, our publications promote progressive leadership and management practices, socially responsible approaches to business, and humane and effective organizations. At the societal level, our publications advance social and economic justice, shared prosperity, sustainability, and new solutions to national and global issues.

A major theme of our publications is "Opening Up New Space." They challenge conventional thinking, introduce new ideas, and foster positive change. Their common quest is changing the underlying beliefs, mindsets, and structures that keep generating the same cycles of problems, no matter who our leaders are or what improvement programs we adopt.

We strive to practice what we preach—to operate our publishing company in line with the ideas in our books. At the core of our approach is *stewardship*, which we define as a deep sense of responsibility to administer the company for the benefit of all of our "stakeholder" groups: authors, customers, employees, investors, service providers, and the communities and environment around us.

We are grateful to the thousands of readers, authors, and other friends of the company who consider themselves to be part of the "BK Community." We hope that you, too, will join us in our mission.

A BK Life Book

This book is part of our BK Life series. BK Life books change people's lives. They help individuals improve their lives in ways that are beneficial for the families, organizations, communities, nations, and world in which they live and work. To find out more, visit www. bk-life.com.

Be Connected

Visit Our Website

Go to www.bkconnection.com to read exclusive previews and excerpts of new books, find detailed information on all Berrett-Koehler titles and authors, browse subject-area libraries of books, and get special discounts

Subscribe to Our Free E-Newsletter

Be the first to hear about new publications, special discount offers, exclusive articles, news about bestsellers, and more! Get on the list for our free e-newsletter by going to www.bkconnection.com

Get Quantity Discounts

Berrett-Koehler books are available at quantity discounts for orders of ten or more copies. Please call us toll-free at (800) 929-2929 or email us at bkp.orders@aidcvt.com

Host a Reading Group

For tips on how to form and carry on a book reading group in your workplace or community, see our website at www.bkconnection.com

Join the BK Community

Thousands of readers of our books have become part of the "BK Community" by participating in events featuring our authors, reviewing draft manuscripts of forthcoming books, spreading the work about their favorite books, and supporting our publishing program in other ways. If you would like to join the BK Community, please contact us at bkcommunity@bkpub.com